CONSTRUCTION MANAGEMENT
FOR PUBLIC AGENCY PROFESSIONALS

Al Palumbo

Al Palumbo

Construction Management for Public Agency Professionals

Copyright © 2013 Al Palumbo

All rights reserved.
ISBN-13: 978-1480159976
ISBN-10: 1480159972

DEDICATION

This book is dedicated to two dear friends for their support and suggestions. *William J. Joyce*, former adjunct professor at New York University, but more importantly the most knowledgeable professional I know in the construction business, and *Angelo Giordani*, whose support and encouragement over the years has given me keen insight into how the world really works.

CONTENTS

	Acknowledgments	i
1	The Construction Process	3
2	Construction Technology	27
3	Procurement of Professional Services	55
4	Affirmative Action	85
5	Construction Contract Law	105
6	Project Labor	121
7	Project Controls	129
8	The Construction Manager	155
9	Quality Assurance	185
10	Construction Safety	197
11	Sustainability	217
12	Leadership	235

ACKNOWLEDGMENTS

I would like to acknowledge the unwavering support of my wife Anna and my daughter Cristina, both of whom have put up with me in pursuit of a long and demanding career, but most importantly have supported me in every endeavor, including the writing of this book.

Chapter 1
The Construction Process

Public Works

Before we begin our discussion of the construction process, let's define a few terms. The first is **public works**. Simply defined, public works are capital improvements in the public infrastructure. This leads to our second term, **infrastructure**. Infrastructure is basic facilities and systems that serve our country, state, cities and towns. In construction it refers to the structures that are needed in order for society to function and for the economy to operate. Thus our roads, highway and bridges provide the conveyance to deliver goods and services required by industry and the population, our schools educate our children, and our hospitals heal the sick. These are the "commons" or the resources available to everyone in our society.

In the public sector, the administration and management of publicly funded construction is performed by professionals of many diverse backgrounds. Some are trained and licensed architects and engineers, others are construction managers. Some have had experience in construction in the field and others have designed projects with little experience in hands on construction. Then there are other public agency professionals with no background in construction, who have been called upon to assist in the public management of a project. Who are these people? They can be lawyers, accountants, investigators, law enforcement, contract administrators, facility managers, senior executives and managers of non-construction agencies, and other types of personnel too numerous to list.

Some agencies have the mission and function to construct facilities. These are easy to identify by their names. Examples are:

Department of Transportation, Department of Public Works, General Services Administration, School Construction Authority, Other agencies generally have their facilities constructed for them by a public agency that builds for other agencies, or they have a design and construction department and build for themselves.

Construction activity impacts on all agencies, and those professionals within dedicated construction agencies or other public agencies that will require construction services all have professionals and managers that may be called upon to support or assist in the delivery of a new construction project.

Wherever you may find yourself, this chapter will provide a starting point to understand construction management basics in the public sector.

The building of infrastructure is the end result of the Construction Process. This process takes months, years, sometimes decades to complete. When the decision is made to build because the funds have been appropriated and allocated, the delivery system for the project must be chosen.

Project Delivery System

The **delivery system** for the project is the way in which the project will be designed, constructed and delivered to the Owner. The most traditional delivery system is the design of the project by the Owner's architectural and engineering design team, the preparation of the bidding documents by the Owner or its Construction Manager, and bidding the work to the general contractor and multiple prime contractors.

Another way to bid the project is to engage a Construction Manager who will be the agent of the Owner (the public agency). The Agency will bid the work through the Construction Manager, who will control all aspects of the project. In this delivery system, the Construction Manager, as the agent of the Owner, has no construction risk. Costs are expected to be controlled, but the Construction Manager will not have the financial responsibility for the project's cost.

Sometimes, agencies will bid the work "at risk". In this case, the Construction Manager bears the responsibility for costs, and must bring the project in at a guaranteed maximum price.

There is also a "design-build" delivery system where there is only one entity responsible to the Owner for the project. This is the design build team of architects, engineers, contractors and subcontractors. Again, the financial responsibility of the design build team is to guarantee the price and bring the project in within budget.

There are other delivery systems that can be used, which are variations of the ones described, but in the end, public construction projects have been created because there is a need that has not been fulfilled. Existing facilities are in disrepair, are outdated, or have reached the end of their useful life expectancy. New facilities are required to meet a demand. Whatever the delivery system, the process is the same: plan the project, fund the project, select the site, design, bid, award the contract and start building.

The Capital Construction Plan

The start of the process of a large public works project begins with the **Capital Construction Plan**. This includes the proposed purchase, construction of demolition of buildings, utilities, highways, bridges, and other infrastructure. Public agencies follow various paths in developing its capital plan. Let's illustrate this point by looking at a plan developed in South Dakota, by the state's Department of Transportation. They developed a five year plan to provide an enhanced quality transportation system. First, the physical condition of the infrastructure needed to be assessed by engaging civil and structural engineers to inspect facilities and provide data that would be used to determine a list of needs by priority of service. They developed criteria to do this, and determined that the project must:

- Support economic vitality
- Increase safety and security
- Aid the environment
- Helps to conserve energy
- Enhances modal integration and connectivity
- Preserves the existing system
- Is coordinated with other planned projects

A list of potential projects was drawn up using these criteria and was reviewed by the state's transportation commission, the railroad board, the department of transportation and a multi-agency task force. They were also reviewed by public industry interest groups, other state, local and federal agencies, and the general public.

In another example, the New York City Education Department is always upgrading and modernizing its vast existing school infrastructure. It developed a five year capital needs assessment establishing criteria, following a similar process. This agency's needs are different than that of a transportation agency's, as in the example above. Therefore, the criteria established were different, but the process was the same – establish a *priority of need* so that scarce resources could be put to the best use. Their criteria included the following for their projects. They had to:

- Increase student capacity to meet programs
- Asses building conditions and determine remaining the remaining useful life of each facility
- Correct violations that threatened life, health and safety

Site Acquisition and Selection

Public agencies acquire sites for construction when there is a need to build in a particular location. Typically decisions on site suitability consider the impact on the community, local economic development considerations, the impact on the environment, the cost implications of building, intended social and cultural outcomes, and the suitability of the site for the function of the facility that will be built. Hopefully, the planners will also consider how the facility will integrate itself into the local community.

Agencies must follow existing laws. For example, new development in urban areas are governed by laws and regulations that require consideration of the impact of the location of projects on the quality of life of residents, the environment, sustainability, the cost of the impact on the community, and the impact on economic development.

In recent history, federal, state and local government entities have placed emphasis on sustainability and environmental quality. **Leadership in Energy and Environmental Design (LEED)** consists of various rating systems for the design, construction and operation of high performance "green" buildings. The U.S. Green

Building Council developed LEED to provide building Owners and operators with a specific basis for determining practical and quantitative green building design, construction, operation and maintenance solutions. Sustainable design and energy efficiency, along with attaining LEED ratings, has become increasingly important elements of new public construction projects, and sustainability starts with site selection. Sites are selected that will have the least amount of impact resulting from construction of the building or infrastructure, and the project will integrate with existing infrastructure, including public transportation, to minimize the use of private transportation alternatives.

There are, of course, other considerations in selecting sites for construction. There is the issue of obtaining multiple returns on investment. The project should contribute to the community through physical improvements, a positive impact on the local economy, and provide an overall public benefit.

For example, New York City's Economic Development Corporation was created to provide opportunities for new businesses and the creation of new jobs to vitalize neighborhoods throughout the city. The corporation acquired a site to build a new five story complex in Brooklyn called the Sunset Park Marketplace. The site contained 1.93 million square feet of space and included a vacant industrial complex and adjacent properties. The intent in acquiring this site was to spur economic development by developing retail and providing needed services, creates construction jobs, create permanent retail jobs, produce tax revenue for the city, and revitalize the Sunset Park neighborhood as part of the renaissance of the borough of Brooklyn. It solicited for a developer to bid on acquisition of the site and to create a project that met the goals of the corporation.

Government has the power to take over private property for the general good of the public and for a public purpose, even if the property owner objects. This is called **Eminent Domain**. This is rooted in the Fifth Amendment of the U.S. Constitution, which provides for the taking of property for public use if the Owner is "justly compensated" (usually fair market value for the property). A public use can be virtually anything sanctioned by a political jurisdiction. Projects include housing, roads, parks, schools, hospitals, and derelict properties that have been abandoned or contribute to "urban blight". Sometimes the process is called "condemnation" or "expropriation".

In the 1960's, Eminent Domain was used for Urban Renewal projects across the country. The intention was to revitalize decaying inner cities and often involved massive demolition including slum clearance. Urban Renewal was very controversial. Public builders like New York's Robert Moses often divided neighborhoods and condemned massive amounts of property to build new highways and expressways, particularly in the Bronx, Brooklyn and Queens. Moses was criticized for his "preference of automobiles to people" as Robert Caro stated in his biography of Moses, The Power Broker: Robert Moses and the Fall of New York

Building Codes

Governmental entities promulgate building codes for their respective jurisdictions. These set minimum standards for construction; their purpose is to protect life, health, and safety of the public and building occupants. The Agency's design team must comply with the applicable building code when they are designing for the Agency's project. There may be regulations that apply to particular types of structures such as schools and hospitals, public assembly spaces, and multiple dwellings. In the United States, there is no national building code. There are, however, model building codes that jurisdictions often adapt. Some examples are: The Building Officials Code Administrators International (BOCA), the International Building Code (IDC), the Uniform Building Code (UBC), and regional codes such as the Southern Building Code Congress International (SBCCI). There are also specialized codes for mechanical and electrical construction, including the Uniform Plumbing Code, the Uniform Mechanical Code, the National Electric Code, the American Society of Heating, Refrigeration and Air-conditioning Engineers (ASHRAE), and others. When the Agency commissions its design team, part of the services that are being purchased is compliance with any and all applicable building codes. Code deficient design results in errors and omissions that are not acceptable.

Each political jurisdiction will adopt or write those codes that it deems necessary for construction. Typically, building codes will also define occupancy groups for buildings. The International Building Code (IBC) addresses requirements succinctly for theatres, businesses, school buildings, day care facilities, industrial buildings, institutional buildings, and utility buildings. This is done so that codes are realistic in terms of building use. For example, a warehouse that stores non-combustible materials does not have to meet the same standards as a hospital.

Zoning

Zoning places legal restrictions on the types of buildings that can be constructed in particular areas. Zoning requirements determine how much undeveloped land can be improved upon through construction, and establishes building set back requirements, parking space requirements, how tall a building can be, and the type of use of the facility that is allowable for a particular block and lot.

Planning Commissions and Boards

Related to zoning are Planning Commission or Planning Board reviews. These entities administer uniform land use review procedures, special permitting, special authorizations, and may also provide for environmental quality reviews. They also grant zoning variances and administrative appeals when it is deemed to be in the public good.

The Building Department

Jurisdictions often have building departments or units that perform the function of a building department. They approve plans for new buildings, and for the alteration of existing buildings. They issue work and equipment permits, building permits, and crane operation permits. They may also issue licenses for master plumbers, welders, operating engineers, riggers, and other trades.

Environmental Protection

All jurisdictions regulate the impact of construction on the environment. Municipalities, townships and county governments may have environmental protection agencies, including bureaus of water supply and sewers. Wherever the function of compliance is housed, these agencies provide for environmental quality reviews, requirements and monitoring of sewer and water connections from mains in the street to buildings, and issue certificates of operation for fossil fuel equipment and other activities that may come under their jurisdictions.

Transportation

Transportation agencies oversee the placement of materials or equipment on the streets and roads within its jurisdiction. These agencies can be state agencies or municipal or local departments of transportation or public works. They issue street opening and closing permits needed for construction operations, sidewalk construction permits, and certifications that work performed in streets or on roads are satisfactory.

Fire Department

Municipal fire departments oversee various aspects of construction that fall within their jurisdiction. These include blasting permits, fuel storage approval, fire detection and electrical systems approval, fire prevention and suppression code compliance including sprinkler systems layouts and other permits.

Americans with Disability Act

When the Congress enacted the Americans with Disabilities Act of 1990 (ADA), it required accessibility for physical challenged individuals, as a civil right. The intent is to allow anyone, regardless of disability, to participate in activities and receive services that are available to the general public. Title II of the ADA requires state and local governments to make all of their programs and services accessible to persons with disabilities. When public facilities are altered and it affects the usability of, or access to the area of the facility that contains a "primary function", an accessible path of travel must be provided to the altered area. Additionally, restrooms, telephones and drinking fountains serving the altered area must be accessible to eth extent that the cost is not "disproportionate" to the cost of the overall alteration. Given the amount of interpretation this can lead to, there have been many court cases that address compliance with the ADA. For example, when a state courthouse in Tennessee added floors to its facility that could not be accessed by persons with physical disabilities, a lawsuit ensued. In Tennessee v. Lane (2004) plaintiffs sued on the grounds that they were being denied access to the court solely because of their disabilities. The U.S. Supreme Court ruled that the plaintiffs' rights were protected under the due process provisions of the 14th Amendment of the U.S. Constitution, and that remedies required by the state were not unreasonable. The state was required to make "reasonable accommodations" to allow disabled persons to exercise their fundamental rights of access to services.

The ADA regulations cover many aspects of construction, including parking, site accessible routes, entrances, rooms and spaces including assemble areas, toilet rooms and bathrooms, special fixtures that include signage, alarms, detectable warnings, and many other requirements. The architect and engineer that design projects for public agencies must be very knowledgeable of ADA requirements and ensure that the design that is provided for construction complies with these requirements.

Construction Plans

The Agency's design team of architects and engineers are supported by dozens of organizations that are instrumental in assisting design by providing standards and resources for the development of construction plans, including drawings and specifications. These organizations distribute information on materials and methods of construction to the design community continuously.

The American Society for Testing and Materials (ASTM) establishes standard specifications for materials commonly used in construction. These specifications have been accepted throughout the United States, and are referred to by number (e.g. ASTM C150 for Portland cement). These numbers are typically used in construction specifications for specific buildings. These designate the quality of material required for the construction. The *Annual Book of ASTM Standards* covers 15 sections of interest plus a master index:

- Iron and Steel Products
- Nonferrous Metal Products
- Metals Test Methods and Analytical Procedures
- Construction
- Petroleum Products, Lubricants, and Fossil Fuels
- Paints, Related Coatings, and Aromatics
- Textiles
- Plastics
- Rubber
- Electrical Insulation and Electronics

- Water and Environmental Technology
- Nuclear, Solar, and Geothermal Energy
- Medical Devices and Services
- General Methods and Instrumentation
- General Products, Chemical Specialties, and End Use Products

Certain materials that are to be installed on a project must be tested before, during or after construction, and there will be outlined in the specifications. Tests are performed by an independent testing laboratory.

Following are some of the key organizations that support the design effort in the United States:

Industry Organizations that Support Design

Underwriters' Laboratories (UL) is a non profit corporation that functions to establish, maintain and operate laboratories that investigate materials, devices, equipment and products, as well as methods of construction. When a product meets UL standards a UL seal of approval is attached to the product.

The **American National Standards Institute (ANSI)** functions to facilitate the development of national standards. ANSI includes technical, professional and trade organizations and private companies, and this organization provides accreditation for standards in the industry, governing the various construction processes.

Construction trade and professional associations, building materials manufacturers, and building contractor organizations also provide important information and play critical roles in the development of construction plans and construction methods by developing technical standards.

The **American Association of Architects (AIA)** is a professional organization of architects offering education, government advocacy, community redevelopment, and public outreach to support the architectural profession, and works with the design and construction community to help coordinate design and construction standards and practices. The AIA has prepared more than 100 forms and contracts that comprise AIA Contract Documents. These forms and contracts were prepared in consultation with Owners, contractors, attorneys, architects, engineers, and others, and are widely used, mostly for private sector construction, and are widely recognized as the industry standard.

The American Society of Civil Engineers (ASCE) is a professional organization of civil engineers, and is the oldest national engineering society in the United States. The ASCE is an ANSI accredited standards development organization that produces consensus standards. The ASCE also publishes civil engineering information and disseminates information widely throughout the industry. It also provides peer reviews of public agencies and projects at the request of the agencies.

The American Society of Mechanical Engineers (ASME) produces codes and standards for technical areas of mechanical systems such as boilers and pressure vessels. The ASME is one of the oldest standards-developing organizations in the world. It produces approximately 600 codes and standards, covering many technical areas, such as boiler components, elevators, measurement of fluid flow in closed conduits, cranes, hand tools, fasteners, and machine tools.

The Institute of Electrical and Electronics Engineers or IEEE is another association of professionals for technology and standards related to electricity. It develops industrial standards for electrical power, energy, telecommunications, consumer electronics, and transportation.

The Construction Specifications Institute (CSI) provides a MasterFormat™ standard. The CSI includes building professionals and members of the construction industry. There are also Trade Associations such as the Western Wood Products Association, a trade association among hundreds that provides research on products that it produces, and establishes standards of product quality. For many years, CSI specifications consisted of 16 Divisions of construction, listed below. In 2010, the MasterFormat provided for an expansion to 50 Divisions, to reflect the increasing complexity of construction.

MasterFormat Specifications Group Original 16 Divisions

- Division 01 — General Requirements
- Division 02 — Existing Conditions
- Division 03 — Concrete
- Division 04 — Masonry
- Division 05 — Metals
- Division 06 — Wood, Plastics, and Composites
- Division 07 — Thermal and Moisture Protection
- Division 08 — Openings
- Division 09 — Finishes
- Division 10 — Specialties
- Division 11 — Equipment
- Division 12 — Furnishings
- Division 13 — Special Construction
- Division 14 — Conveying Equipment
- Division 15 — Mechanical Systems
- Division 16 — Electrical Systems

It is useful to understand how each of the major divisions is described, because these form the outline of specifications that will be contained in bidding documents and the final construction contract.

General requirements: Specifications that address aspects of the project that are the responsibility of the general contractor, and may be found in the General Conditions or special conditions.

Site Work: All work performed on the site, including clearing, grading, excavating, drainage, site utilities, roadways, walkways, underpinning and landscaping.

Concrete: Concrete formwork, precast concrete, cast-in-place concrete and reinforcing concrete.

Masonry: Mortar, units of masonry, stone, and the restoration of masonry.

Metals: Structural steel, metal stud and joist systems, miscellaneous metals, ornamental metals, and other related items.

Carpentry: Materials made of wood and materials used for wood framing. It includes rough and finish carpentry.

Moisture Protection: Waterproofing, thermal insulation, roofing materials, skylights, flashing, caulking and sealants.

Doors, Windows and Glass: Doors and windows, finish hardware, glass, curtain walls, window walls, storefront systems, and weather-stripping.

Specialties: Items that require prefabrication and items that are proprietary. For example, items under this category include signs, fire place equipment, toilet accessories, moveable partitions, and chalk boards.

Equipment: A very wide range of equipment applicable to commercial, educational, laboratory, medical, restaurant, residential and other types of construction. Examples are laboratories, cabinets, refrigerators, kitchen cabinetwork, and countertops.

Furnishings: Artwork, prefabricated fixtures, carpeting, furniture, work stations, blinds, drapes and shades.

Special Construction: Special purpose rooms, prefabricated structures, and other items such as swimming pools.

Conveying Systems: Elevators, escalators, lifts, hoists, materials handling systems, and the like.

Mechanical Systems: Plumbing systems, heating systems, fire extinguishing systems, air conditioning systems, and refrigeration.

Electrical Systems: Electrical services and distribution systems, lighting, communications, electrical power equipment, and electrical hearing and cooling systems.

Blueprints

The term "blueprint" came about because drawings were printed as white lines on a blue background. When plans were drawn by hand, they were drawn on vellum (film like paper that is semi transparent) and were processed and treated with ammonia, and were actually produced in blue. With increasing use of computer software such as AutoCAD and Micro Station, drawings are no longer drawn by hand by most designers and are easier to produce, and more accurate if properly prepared. Although in many cases, electronic means of producing drawings have replaced this method of production, the term blueprint survives and is used to mean prints or drawings. Construction plans also convey views of the project. Thus, when looking at a floor plan, site plan or foundation plan, you are viewing the project from directly above. The views that construction drawings provide are of the front, the back and the sides. The top view is called the plan view. The front, side and back views are called elevations. A view of the interior of a building structure or element is called a section.

The larger the project, the more complex the plans that need to be produced. For the construction of a facility or building, the set of plans will be in accordance with the type of construction involved:

A – Architectural. Architectural plans include plot plan, elevations, framing and building details.

S- Structural. Structural plans depict the superstructure, consisting of steel, concrete or wood.

M – Mechanical. Mechanical plans depict heating, ventilation and air conditioning (HVAC).

E – Electrical. Electrical plans include power and lighting systems. Electrical subsystems include fiber optics, fire alarm, telecommunications, security, etc.

U – Utility. Utility plans include civil engineering plans for public utility systems such as water supply from the city main to the building line, electrical supply, and other utilities to the building.

P -Plumbing. Plumbing plans include waste and water supply systems. Plans are arranged in the order of project construction.

Plans will be labeled by discipline and they will be numbered. Examples include: civil engineering (C-1, C-2, etc), structural Engineering (S-1, S-2, etc.), Architectural (A-1, A-2, etc.), electrical

(E-1. E-2, etc.), mechanical (M-1, M-2, etc.) and plumbing (P-2. P-2, etc.)

Project Phases

A public agency construction project undergoes various phases before the project is delivered to the Agency. Typically these are known as:

- Design phase (including pre-design planning)
- Bid and award phase
- Construction phase

Design Phase

In this phase the Agency procures and selects a design team. Often, if the project requires an architectural lead, the request for proposal will be issued to architectural firms, and these consultants will assemble a team including the civil engineer, structural engineer, mechanical engineer, electrical engineer and any special consultants based on the requirements of the advertised scope of work.

For solicitations that are heavy infrastructure, such as highway, bridge and other civil works, the solicitation is directed at civil and structural engineering firms as the lead, and they will follow a similar process of assembling a team based on requirements, such as landscape architects, land surveyors and other team members.
In this phase, the design team will design and produce the construction contract documents, consisting of drawings or plans, specifications and contract documents that will be bid to general contractors.

Typically on building projects, the selected architect will work with the Agency Project Manager, representing the Owner, to identify the Owner's needs, developing a scope of work reflecting these needs, and will then proceed to prepare a conceptual or schematic design, which is best described as "preliminary". This phase allows for an order of magnitude determination for costs that are at this phase "ball park" because the details of the project have not yet been established through the design and approval process. **Order of Magnitude** or "rough estimates" are always at the front of project preparation. They will provide a range of costs so that the size and scope of the proposed project can begin to become quantified. The estimates prepared at this level are based on the experience of the design team's estimator based on similar types of work, market conditions, and other historical information. Scope decisions may be influenced at this stage by these rough estimates. The estimates may be prepared in response to budget planning and appropriation requests for proposed construction some time in the future.

Before construction starts, it is important to obtain detailed cost estimates. These will be prepared before work is bid to general contractors, and may be produced at different stages of the completion of design. For example, an estimate at 30% of design will allow for decisions about the project scope and methods of construction before the design progresses too far. Once decisions are made at this stage, other estimates may be required at 60%, 90%, or 100% so project costs can be monitored all the way up to bid. The final estimate will be based on 100% completion of construction documents and should be used as a control estimate for the comparison of bids that are received.

The detailed estimate will give the specific breakdown of project costs. Estimates become more refined and accurate as the design team fully investigates existing building conditions for rehabilitation projects, and as details about the full scope for such items as the building systems, building envelope, potential hazardous materials, and various interior element can be completed.

Upon acceptance of the order of magnitude estimate, drawings progress in stages, and the drawings will serve to explain how the project will be built. Later on, the drawings will be combined with contract specifications, general and supplemental conditions and other documents, and will become the construction contract documents. Anyone who is involved in planning, supplying and building the project needs to be able to read and interpret the architectural and engineering plans, or construction drawings.

Schematic design is a very critical and important phase because expectations are identified, budgets and schedules are established, funding through allocations of existing funding or new appropriations are put into motion. The general scope, the preliminary design, the scale and the relationships of the entire project components are tied together. The outcome must be a project that has a clear definition, with a comprehensive scope of work, budget and schedule. Schematic level drawings will be provided by the key design team members including the architect and the various engineering disciplines.

The technical group within the Agency will be reviewing and reacting to the schematic design. The following tasks should be accomplished before or during this phase of design:

Tasks in Schematic Design

- Identify the project team members
- Arrange for review by all stakeholders
- Determine the project schedule
- Determine the site design
- Determine the building design
- Determine the mechanical, electrical, plumbing and fire protection systems
- Outline a commissioning strategy plan
- Determine the project budget
- Reconcile budget with scope
- Prepare project buyout strategy

Design Development. It is in this phase that the design team's services focus on the preparation of the design development documents, consisting of approved schematic design studies for submission to the Agency for approval. In this sub-phase of design, the designer elaborates and refines the design concept and resolves issues that are important to the project. Schematic design drawings are refined to become more detailed and elaborate, and the selection of building materials are finalized.

If this phase is executed properly, the design decision has been made and issues have been coordinated and resolved. It is not advisable to rush design development and move directly into the construction documents sub-phase of design until all issues that can be resolved in this phase are addressed.

During design development, conceptual plans should include:

- Site plan development detailing buildings, roads, parking, site drainage, utilities and landscaping

- Selection of building materials for the building shell and interiors that are best suited for the particular use
- Design development of floor plans, detailing architectural and structural elements, mechanical, electrical and plumbing systems, and outline specifications

Construction Documents. In the Construction Documents phase, a set of contract documents, including drawings and specifications are prepared. These graphically and verbally describe the project, the Agency's preferences and wishes, and define the size, function, organization and aesthetics as intended by the design, and which must be built by the contractor and Construction Manager. These documents will prescribe the engineer's requirements for structural systems and will be submitted to the appropriate entity for permits. The drawings will be used for competitive bidding among contractors so that the bids, construction schedule and project approach can be evaluated.

The plans for building construction will include site plans, structural plans, architectural plans, framing plans, and plans for the building systems including mechanical, electrical and plumbing, These plans are the drawings in the bid set and the contract that accompany corresponding specifications. Descriptions of the plans that are expected at 100% of completion are summarized below.

Civil Engineering plans include site plans, utilities, grading and landscaping, and easements. They typically will show contour lines, driveways, walkways, property lines, setbacks for buildings, and locations of site utilities. The site plan is a drawing based on an existing property.

Land Survey. The site plan must show the location of the proposed structure and all existing buildings in relation to the property lines and each other. Because survey drawings provide the measurement and establish the shape of the site on paper, they become a baseline for the drawing of the site plan.

Site grading plans are drawings of the property which indicates the grading, drainage pattern and elevations of the foundation. All dimensions and elevations are either in the Metric or English system.

Structural plans will show foundation, walls, footings and piers, structural steel, the support system required for the building, and the roof framing system. Also shown are foundation and basement plans. Details and section drawings will also be included in the structural set.

Architectural plans depict floor plans, elevations, sections, detail drawings, and schedules for doors, windows, and hardware. Floor plans show walls, doors, stairways, mechanical equipment, and other features, and is prepared for each level of the building. The floor plan should show locations for all floors affected by proposed work. Basement floor plans give further details about the location of footings, load bearing walls, steel rebar concrete reinforcements, and other structural elements the home requires to support the walls and roof.

A cross section of a plan is a cut away view of the building from the footings to the roof. The cross section shows building materials and their relation to each other. Sections are drawn to show the building in a slice. They show items such as walls, stairs, and details that cannot be depicted in other drawings in a clear way.

Architectural plans show *elevations*, or views of the exterior features of the building. If the design is unusual, additional elevation plans will be drawn to show these features of the exterior. Usually, four elevation plans are prepared for a basic structure to show the front, back and sides.

Framing plans include plans required for framing the floors, roof and wall sections.

Electrical plans provide for the electrical and lighting plan, reflected ceiling plans to show lighting, and electrical panel schedules. There may also be riser diagrams showing the distribution of service from floor to floor. Drawings may also include load calculations. On a small job the electrical plan may be overlaid on a floor plan. If required, electrical diagrams are included.

Electrical diagrams usually include a legend or key on the page which explains what each symbol represents. These show the location of electrical outlets, fans, fixtures, light fixtures etc. Electrical diagrams may also include legends for heating systems, door swings and sizes, or even to specify certain finishes.

Mechanical plans include heating, ventilation, and air conditioning (HVAC) plans. Plumbing plans may also be included, or shown as separate plumbing plans. Sprinkler systems are also part of the mechanical drawings set. Schedules for piping and fittings, plumbing fixtures, and HVAC equipment may be included. On a small job, the mechanical plan may be overlaid on a floor plan.

Plumbing plans show the layout for water service, the sewage system, and the location of plumbing fixtures. The complexity of the project will dictate how many drawings are required.

Detail drawings show unique features such as arches and retaining walls.

Schedules are lists of materials needed in the construction process. These drawings will show items, identifications, sizes, numbers required, and will reference the items in the plan and elevation drawings. Examples are: door schedules, window schedules, lighting fixture schedules and finishing schedules.

Blue print reading is beyond the scope of this textbook. It is important to realize that blue print reading requires the skill to visualize the project and interpret what is shown on the drawings. Reading construction prints requires an understanding of the lines and symbols that appear on drawings. These are generally defined so that they can be universally applied by drafters and CAD technicians. Examples are property lines, center line (to show centers of objects like columns and fixtures), dimension lines and break lines. Symbols represent items such as building materials and fixtures. A *legend* will define the symbols for the reader.

Building Information Modeling (BIM)

Building Information Modeling (BIM) is starting to be embraced in construction, and in time it most likely will be used extensively. BIM is a process for generating and managing building data during the life cycle of the building (from construction and use to eventual demolition), using a three dimensional building modeling software in real time, and producing the Building Information Model, including the facility's geometry, spatial relationships, pertinent geographic information, properties and quantities of building components.

BIM offers improved visualization of the facility constructed, and makes it easy to retrieve information about the building. The development and coordination of construction documents will become improved, providing increased delivery of the building, cost efficiencies, and the ability to access information about building components and systems.

Highway, Bridge, Roadway and Utility Construction (Heavy Civil)

So far, we have discussed the construction of buildings and facilities, although much of what has been written applies to the construction of heavy civil infrastructure. This section describes the construction process as it applies to this type of construction project.

Planning Phase

The planning phase for heavy civil construction can come from requests from municipal, local and state agencies, regional planning organizations and others. The length of time required for planning and programming this work depends on a number of factors, such as the proposed functional role of the roadway for regional or local travel, mobility and access, costs, availability of revenue to pay for the project, economic impacts, and support of other agencies such as the Federal Highway Administration (FHA), and other agencies that provide for federally funding. Each state transportation agency, all of whom depend on funding from the FHA, have long range transportation plans with strategic highway and transit goals. In the case of transportation infrastructure, the factors that transportation planners consider in making recommendations include development and land-use plans, traffic patterns, level of service requirements, and safety needs. Build and no-build alternatives are also considered. Environmental impacts and economic impacts also are considered.

The project scoping phase that transportation agencies utilize confirms the purpose and need for the proposed project. The environmental review process is initiated as may be required. The level of environmental documents and the need for water quality permits are determined. Environmental issues are reviewed by experts in the area of noise, air quality, archaeology, architecture, wildlife, and biology.

The project team is established, consisting of internal engineering department personnel, and outside engineering firms, as required. The following tasks are planned and implemented: (a). Holding the initial scoping team meeting; (b). Performing the survey;

(c). Developing the initial design; (d). Considering context sensitive solutions; (e). Evaluating public involvement strategies

As this phase of the project progresses, the project goals and objectives are refined, as is the scope. Typical sections of a roadway are located and determined. This is based on such considerations as the anticipated volume of traffic, the type of roadway, called the functional classification (arterial, local, collector) and the terrain – level, rolling, or mountainous.

Preliminary Design Phase

This phase includes (a). Design of roadway, structures and bridges; (b). Traffic control devices/intelligent transportation systems and landscaping; (c). Determining right of way and utility impacts; (d). Performing "constructability" and work zone reviews; (e). Completing the environmental documents; (f). Holding the public hearing team meeting and public hearing, and (g). Obtaining design approval.

A preliminary design is prepared and reviewed by all stakeholders in the project, such as affected property owners and local governments. The Agency may want to consider alternative schemes, and in this case may conduct informational meetings or public hearings, before making a final decision about the location or features of the roadway. Issues may include the right-of-way width of the roadway, types of interchanges and intersections, construction materials, aesthetics, noise walls for to reduce highway traffic noise, etc. Information meetings and public hearings are advertised in the newspaper and other media, and citizens are provided with a comment period. Once the decision is made to approve the preliminary design, the next phase of design is implemented.

The Detailed Design Phase

In this phase, the following is addressed: (a). Design of roadway, structures and bridges, traffic control devices, intelligent transportation systems, and landscaping; (b). Determining right of way and utility impacts; (c). Developing erosion and sedimentation/hydraulic plans; (d). Performing utility design; (e). Holding the utility field inspection; (f). Authorizing right of way; (g). Performing "constructability" and work zone reviews, and (h). Negotiation for property acquisition via offers of fair market value and appraisals of property value. Property can be acquired through eminent domain if amicable agreement cannot be reached.

The Final Design and Right of Way Acquisition Phase

In this phase, the following tasks are finalized: (a). The design of roadways, structures and bridges, traffic control devices, intelligent transportation systems, and landscaping; (b). Right of way and utility impacts, erosion and sedimentation plans, and utility design; (c). Obtaining environmental permits; (d). Holding the utility field inspection; (e). Authorizing right of way and utilities; (f). Performing "constructability", work zone, and maintenance of traffic/transportation management plan reviews; (g) Holding the pre-advertisement conference team meeting.

Chapter 1 References

The following sources were utilized in writing this chapter:

Baldwin, J. and Clark, K. *There is No Compromise.* Negro Digest. Vol. 12, No. 12 October, 1963.

Leung, R. Eminent Domain: *Being Abused? Is Seizure of Private Property Always in the Public Interest?* July 4, 2004. Retrieved from www.cbsnews.com/.../09/.../main575343.shtml

Madsen, J. *Build Smarter, Faster and Cheaper With BIM.* July, 2008. Retrieved from www.buildings.com

Moses, Paul. *Times to Commoners Go Elsewhere.* July 9, 2005. The Village Voice. Retrieved from www.villagevoice.com.

Cornell University Law School.
http://www.law.cornell.edu/supct/html/02-1667.ZS.html

International building Code (ICC) Website. www.iccsafe.org

The Construction Specifications Institute Website.
http://www.csinet.org/

IEEE Website. http://www.ieee.org

Chapter 2
Construction Technology

Introduction

The Agency is about to begin a construction project to meet a public need. Perhaps the project will address economic development of a neighborhood, transportation, security, education, health, and the general welfare. The next step is the engagement of design professionals to assist the Agency in planning, programming and designing the project. A team of designers – Architects and engineers, will work with the Agency directly or through a Construction Manager or resident engineering firm to consolidate the Agency's ideas about the new project, and will, as the project progresses in this pre-construction stage, assemble the team of experts required working out costs, concepts and details. Drawings and specifications will be produced, consolidated into construction contract documents, and incorporated into bid documents that will be issued to general contractors, who will bid on the work of the project. General contractors, in turn, will engage subcontractors to participate in the bid by submitting quotes. The Agency will go through its bid and award process.

The drawings and specifications will be submitted to government regulatory agencies such as the building department, departments of environmental protection, transportation, public works and other regulatory agencies that will issue the required permits and licenses required to build. The project may now be constructed, entering the construction phase.

The construction contract documents serve as the instruction manual for assembling the project. The construction industry has standardized the way construction specifications (the written instructions for the project) are prepared. The specifications are accompanied by the construction drawings, and these are integrally used together to build the project. In the United States, the Construction Specifications Institute (CSI) maintains and provides standardization of building specifications, and they are provided in a structure and format. Presently the format is presented in "MasterFormat". This is a system for organizing construction specifications.

Competent public agency managers who are engaged in the administration of construction projects have various levels of expertise in construction. Some may be engineers, architects, constructors, have formal training in construction management, or may not have been formally trained prior to being assigned to a project.

The following discussion of construction materials and processes may prove useful to readers with little or no background in basic construction technology and processes. In reading the rest of this book, the following may be helpful in recognizing and understanding the life cycle of a project, various construction terms, and other information related to the actual building process.

The Basics – Building a Simple Project

Let's look at building basics that are involved in a relatively common building structure, a residential home. Of course, your projects are generally much more complex than home construction, but there is a basic process that can give you a pretty good idea of how the building is put together in the field. We will then go on to discuss construction materials and operations on the types of projects you encounter in your jobs every day, so please indulge the author!

The Site

The first step in constructing the project is to find a suitable site that we can build on. Our first consideration will be whether the site contains a buildable lot. This means that the land that will house our building is suitable to support the structure and the utilities that we need to make the building function as designed. In the case of the construction of a simple home, we could expect a competent and experienced builder to construct a simple home of about 2,000 square feet (sf) in about three to four months, with good weather conditions.

To make sure that a site is a good one for our project a soils test is performed to determine drainage and composition of the soil at the building site. A survey establishes property lines and setbacks. The foundation and basement, crawlspace, slab, or pier is laid, with the style depending on site conditions and the Owner's preferences. More on this later as it applies to public construction. If we are building in the country and there are no city sewers or water mains to tie into, we will also be performing percolation tests for the suitability of an on-site septic system, and we will want to know the depth of the water table for an on site well. If we are in the city (or densely populated area), we will be tapping off the sewer main and water main service running down our street.

Framing

Residential homes can be stick built, modular or concrete form. If it is stick built, it means that 2x4 or 2x6 lumber is used to create the structure's skeleton. Roofs will be built using prefabricated trusses which will structurally support the roof during framing. Simple and complex projects can be stick built or contain prefabrication elements found in modularly constructed buildings.

If the building is of modular construction, this means that major sections of the building are being fabricated in a factory, and then shipped to the site for assembly. The advantages of modular construction are that the building can be assembled faster than a stick built structure, and because it is fabricated in a shop, quality control can be improved because fabrication is under better controlled conditions than in the field. The quality variables on this type of building construction primarily come into play in proper assembly of the modular components at the project site.

Mechanicals

The building systems refer to heating, electrical, plumbing, and air conditioning. In order to install the mechanical system, rough-ins are set up before the interior finishes are installed, as these will be the path of travel of the various building systems, and it would not be smart to build the interior and then demolish parts of the interior to accommodate the building systems. Now, there might be a general contractor that does the foundation, framing and exterior, and the general contractor (GC) may also use subcontractors for part or all of this work. The GC will then usually hire mechanical, electrical and plumbing subcontractors, who will return in the later stages after the rough-ins to install fixtures such as toilets and showers, vent covers, switch plates and other components.

Insulation, Windows and Doors, Drywall

Buildings are insulated from the elements to make the building efficient for heating and cooling. The types of insulation vary, and are referred to as batt, roll, blown-in, etc. Insulation has an R-value, which measures the ability to transfer heat. The type of insulation depends on the type of building, its geographic location, and weather patterns where the building is sited. Quality windows and doors are an important component for energy efficient and secure buildings. Wall finishes are usually done with drywall-gypsum panels that are nailed or screwed to the framing over the installation. They are then taped and textured for uniformity. If they are "rocking the house", this is not a concert, but the process of installing drywall (sheetrock).

Exterior Finishes and Exterior Finishes

The choices for exterior siding, trim, and roofing are numerous and are at the discretion of the Owner. In simple home construction, it may depend on what is common in your area. In home construction, there are hundreds of little details comprising the interior finishes of a home: paint, trim, wallpaper, flooring, cabinets, countertops, appliances, and fixtures, to name just a few. In public construction, multiply this into the thousands!

Walk-Through

Once the construction is completed, your builder will schedule a walk-through, where you will do a final inspection of the home. Now is the time to note anything that is not satisfactory and get a written schedule of when adjustments will be made.

Of course, even the construction of a residential home can be complex, and issues will arise that need to be addressed, so forgive the oversimplification. Hopefully, the point has been made that this is the basic outline for the construction of a simple structure, and can give us some basis for understanding the construction of more complex, public construction.

The Public Project

For projects to be constructed in the public sector, there is long term planning, capital needs assessments, master planning, budget appropriations, a prolonged procurement process, selection of the architect, engineer, contractor, myriads of approvals by regulatory agencies and stakeholders. We will touch on these later.

By its very nature, a public construction project is more complex than building a residential home. As a homeowner, you may go to a builder who already has a site, or you may have your own site. The builder may already have stock plans and models for you to choose from, instead of using an architect.

Let's look at the phases of a more complex construction project in more detail. We will look at the various phases from prepping the site, to the actual building, and along the way we will introduce some technical terms and concepts that you will also be dealing with in the administration of a construction project.

Site Work

Earthwork

In order for construction to occur on a selected site, it is necessary to prepare the site to receive the new facility, whether it is a building, highway or other construction type. The site needs to be brought to grades required for the structures that will be built. Earthwork refers to construction activity necessary to bring the site to rough grading, as required in the specifications and shown on the drawings. Every type of project requires earthwork. In order to assure that the soil conditions are sufficient for proposed construction, field soil and laboratory testing is performed on existing soil to determine suitability for construction.

The soil report prepared by the geotechnical engineer (a civil engineer that specializes in soils) contains information that is critical to the designer, who will use this to determine the types of materials that need to be used. Soil test borings or subsurface investigation is performed, and soils at different depths are tested in the lab. The soils are classified by type, and in designing foundations and footings for structures, it must be determined that the soils will bear the load of the building without causing instability in the future.

It is also important to determine other site conditions through exploration, including the existence of bedrock and the level of the water table. Building codes specify the allowable bearing pressure for different soil types. They specify how many ponds can be supported by one square foot of soil.

Excavation

A certain level of excavation is required during the development of the site. Organic topsoil is fine for growing tomatoes but is not a good building material because it decomposes shrinks and swells based on its moisture content. After the top soil is removed, digging continues in order to place footings below the level where the ground freezes, known as the frost line. This is because soil expands when it freezes and the force can actually lift a building and cause extensive damage. Where there is a lot of rock on the site, excavation is costly and slower. If the rock cannot be removed with a reasonable effort using machinery, blasting is often necessary if its use is practical, depending on where the project is located.

The edges of excavations are often sloped so that the soil does not slide back into the excavated area. Sheeting is a temporary wall that is constructed to hold back the soil. Sheet piling uses vertical planks of wood, steel or precast concrete placed tightly against one another and driven into the earth to create a solid wall before excavation begins.

A slurry wall is a more expensive and complex form of sheeting that is used mostly when it becomes part of the permanent foundation wall of a building. A trench is excavated to create a form for each wall. The trench is kept full of slurry (water mixture of insoluble materials) at all times. The slurry prevents the trench from collapsing by providing outward pressure, balancing inward hydraulic forces and preventing water flow into the trench. Reinforcement is then lowered in and the trench is filled with concrete, which displaces the slurry.

Seismic Considerations

Some areas are prone to earthquake activity. This seismic activity causes vibration of the ground, starting at the epicenter and proceeding in waves, much like the waves generated by throwing a pebble into a pond. Government entities require special precautions that will allow buildings, bridges and other structures to withstand seismic forces in constructing soil structures and foundations.

Dewatering

In order to build, it is sometimes necessary to modify water site conditions at the project site. Dewatering is a process used when a site must be made free of water. This is required when excavation is below the existing water table. Water is usually pumped out using sump pumps. Well points may be used to depress the water table. These are created with vertical pieces of pipe that have screened openings at the base, allowing water to enter while keeping soil out. These are connected to pipes leading to the pumps to draw down the water table in the area of excavation. The subsequent control of water beneath the earth's surface, referred to as "subterranean water" is addressed in the foundation and site design by the civil engineer.

Soil Density

Compaction of soils is necessary in order to achieve soil density. This is done as part of site preparation so that the new facility will not cause too much settlement. Soil settles when a load is placed on it because air and water are released when the soil is compressed.

If soils are not properly compacted and allowed to settle, settlement can occur after construction. The author was an Owner's representative on a state supported housing project that had been built years before without sufficient compaction. In the original construction, site utilities were pile supported. As the site began to settle, electric duct banks and water main structures began to emerge like speed bumps in the road as the surrounding roadway settled. Sanitary and domestic water lines began to shear at the building line of high rise and town house structures. In this case, the fix came fifteen years after the original construction, at a high price.

Foundation

Once a site is mapped out on a site plan, excavation operations can begin after the site has been cleared of trees and brush (grubbing), previous structures and other natural or physical structures. After the survey of a site, heavy equipment is brought in to begin excavation of the location of the foundation, at the specified depth. Footings are installed according to the foundation plan, and the depth of the footing must be below the line where frost will go down into the soil at the peak of low winter temperatures. This is referred to as the frost line.

Footings will usually either be formed in a trench dug into the ground or will be formed in an open pit where the structure will be placed. The depth of the footing must be below the frost line. All foundation types are protected from ground moisture through the construction of drainage systems and capillary breaks and vapor barriers.

The part of a building structure that is below the surface is the foundation. The foundation functions to transfer the structural loads of the building or structure safely into the ground. Any type of building structure needs a foundation to support it. A house needs a greater foundation than a backyard shed. An even larger building made of concrete and steel weighs much more than a house and must reach the quality of soil or rock that can carry a far greater load. Foundation design must take into account the stability of the soil, underground water conditions, and rock below the surface.

The foundation will provide a base that will remain stable to support the entire structure. The foundation must support dead loads (such as the weight of the building itself) live loads (people that occupy the facility), wind loads, horizontal pressures of earth and water against the foundation structure, uplift forces from underground water, horizontal and vertical forces produced by earthquakes and tremors. A foundation, in order to be satisfactory, must not settle in a manner that will destabilize the building it supports, and must be feasible and practical to build without impacting adversely on adjacent structures.

Most shallow foundations are simple concrete footings. A column footing consists of a square block of concrete that accepts the load coming from above by a building column. The load is then spread across an area of soil that can manage the bearing stress caused by the load. A wall footing is a continuous strip of concrete that serves the same function for a load bearing wall that is supporting the structure. Deep foundations are more complicated foundations. Concrete piers, called caissons are used when there is sufficient rock or load bearing soil to accept and support the stress from the structure being supported by the foundation. A caisson's function is much like a column footing because it spreads the load from a column over a large enough area. Shafts are sunk to the required depth and filled with concrete. This is constructed as a watertight chamber and is used when there is water or water bearing soil conditions.

Pile foundations are used to carry and transfer the load of the building or structure to the bearing ground that is located at some depth below the surface. The pile foundation basically consists of the pile cap and the piles. Piles are long and slender, unlike caissons, and are driven into the earth rather than drilled and poured. Pile members are made of different materials such as structural steel H piles, precast concrete piles, cylinder piles of concrete cylindrical sections, composite piles consisting of wood and cast-in-place concrete, wood piles, and sheet piling, which may be made of wood, pre-stressed concrete or steel. Piles are used so that low bearing capacity soil can be bypassed to reach deeper soil or rock with higher bearing capacity. The object is to reach soil that will be able to support the weight and structure of the building.

Underpinning

Underpinning is performed in order to strengthen and stabilize foundations of an existing building. It is required when existing foundations are not adequate for supporting the building loads that they are carrying, leading to excessive settlement of the building over time. Changes in the use of the building, or additions, overload the existing foundations, leading to settlement and destabilization. New construction near a building may disturb the soil around the foundations or require that its foundations be carried deeper, through underpinning.

The author was associated with the Second Avenue Subway Project in New York City. Underpinning was required to stabilize many buildings lining Second Avenue in the area of the launch box for the tunnel boring machine. Many of these buildings were built around the 1900's or before, on rubble type fill. Blasting, pile driving, and tunnel excavation up to a 60 foot depth have taken their toll on the foundations of some of these buildings and they needed to be stabilized. Underpinning, while necessary in cases like this, is a slow, expensive, and specialized process.

Retaining Walls

A retaining wall holds back soil to create a change in the elevation of the ground in order to resist pressure from the earth that bears against it on its uphill side. These are constructed of varying materials, including preservative treated wood, masonry, precast concrete, concrete poured at the site, and galvanized steel.

Waterproofing and Drainage

Groundwater threatens a building's substructure, especially where the site contains a high water table or poorly draining soil. Groundwater can intrude into the best constructed concrete wall and undermine it, let alone basement walls that are usually imperfect.

The way to waterproof the substructure is usually through installation of a drainage system or waterproof membrane. Drainage is designed to reduce the amount of water that makes its way to foundations, and a waterproof membrane serves as a barrier to the path of water traveling toward the basement wall. Drainage is a relatively easy installation process that prevents the buildup of water pressure that will undermine slabs and basement walls. Methods include gravel drains and the use of drainage mats manufactured of inert fibers or other porous materials. A filter fabric prevents fine soil particles from entering and clogging the drainage passages in the mat, so that subterranean water will fall though the porous material to a drain pipe at the footing carrying the water away from the structure. There are other drainage systems for below slab and above slab drainage using perforated pipe in crushed stone and sump and pump systems.

Backfilling

After the basement walls are waterproofed and insulation is installed to retard heat loss, all drainage features are completed, and internal construction to support basement walls, such as interior walls and floors have been installed, its time to backfill the area around the substructure. This is done to restore the level of the ground by placing soil back against the outside of the basement walls, compacting it in layers.

Concrete

Concrete is a rock like construction material composed by mixing coarse and fine aggregates, Portland cement, and water and allowing the mixture to harden. Heat is produced as the cement combines chemically (hydration) with water to form strong crystals that bind the aggregates together. Many people misuse the word "cement" when they really mean to say "concrete". Concrete is used for pavement, architectural structures, foundations, highways, bridges, walls, footings, and many other structures. It is used more than any other man made material. Concrete cures over many days, and the longer it cures, the stronger it becomes.

As a public administrator, it is important to be aware that the architect or engineer engaged by the agency has developed plans and specifications for concrete work, and that there are standards for the material, including the way it is supposed to be installed (means and methods), the ambient temperature required by the manufacturer during installation and other requirements. The agency is most likely to engage a Resident Engineer or Construction Manager who will supervise installation and monitor quality, to ensure that the work is being performed in accordance with standard industry practices, meets code, and is in accordance with the specifications. Material testing will also be required, and between material testing and inspection for quality, these are the primary means to ensure that the public entity is receiving the product it has paid for, and is obtaining quality.

Here are some terms associated with concrete:

Portland cement – the most common type of cement that includes concrete, mortar and plaster.

Mix design – the correct mix of the cementitious materials. The mix design is based on the type of structure that is being formed with concrete.

Limestone – a mixture of oxides of calcium, silicon and aluminum. The limestone is heated with clay and similar materials to make Portland cement.

Aggregates – fine and coarse aggregates are a large portion of the concrete mixture, such as sand and crushed stone. Green construction uses recycled aggregates.

Reinforcement – Concrete has no useful tensile strength. Tensile strength means the force required to pull something to the point where it will break. Materials like rope, wire and structural beams have tensile strength. Therefore, without the ability to reinforce concrete with structural steel, a concrete structure would literally tear itself apart as it contracts and expands with temperature changes. Fortunately, concrete adheres to steel and they are both chemically compatible. If steel is placed where there are tensile forces in a structural member, concrete will be able to resist compressive forces and the combination provides strong structural support. Concrete is strong when it is in compression. Compressive strength means the capacity of the concrete to withstand "pushing" forces. Compressive strength in concrete is tested to determine that the concrete is strong enough to do the job. Rebar, or reinforcement bar, is installed in concrete because while concrete is strong in compression, it is weak in tension because cement that holds aggregate in place can crack. Reinforced concrete solves this problem by adding metal reinforcing bars, glass fiber, or plastic fiber to carry tensile loads. Think of tensile loads as a "pulling" force.

Concrete slump test– This measures the "workability" of concrete. Workability refers to the ability of fresh concrete mix to fill forms and molds properly without compromising quality, and depends on water content, aggregate, concrete and the level of hydration. The *concrete slump test* measures the plasticity of a fresh batch of concrete. Concrete is measured using an Abrams Cone and the concrete in the cone must slump to a certain level due to gravity. It must meet ASTM test standards.

Prestressing– Concrete is very strong in compression, usually rated up to 2,500 pounds per square inch (PSI), but it's relatively weak in tension. This means that concrete can be prone to cracking due to deflection, or bending. When a beam supports a load, the compressive side of the beam is squeezed slightly and the tension side is stretched with a similar force. The steel of the beam will stretch under tension due to tensile strength, but the concrete around it will crack from the edge of the beam. If the steel beam encased in concrete is given more tensile strength, there will be less force exerted on concrete, and there will be little or no cracking of concrete. Prestressed members contain less concrete; they are lighter, and less expensive. In pretensioning, lengths of steel wire or cables are laid in the empty mold and stretched. The concrete is placed, and as it sets, the steel cables are released. This causes the concrete to be placed in compression, as the steel shrinks back to its original size from being stretched. The compressive stresses push back on the tensile bending stresses of an applied load.

Post-tensioning. Post-tension concrete construction creates a tight grid of steel cables that actively help support a reinforced concrete slab. Unlike conventional reinforcement bar (rebar), which is inactive and only helps keep concrete intact after cracking, post-tension tendons continually contribute to structural integrity. Post-tensioning is usually done in the factory. It uses high strength steel strands, known as tendons, that are covered in sheathing to protect them from corrosion and it prevents the tendons from binding with the concrete. They are put into tension after the concrete is formed. A tensile force is exerted on the tendon, and the concrete is compressed with an equal, opposite force. Post-tensioned concrete came into use over 40 years ago. It was originally used primarily for bridge construction, and now includes many building types such as office buildings, parking structures, and more.

Masonry

Masonry refers to hollow and solid units of building materials that are held together by mortar, a workable paste mixture of cement, water and fine aggregate masonry that binds these construction blocks together. These blocks may be stone, brick, cinder block, or other forms of block. Some of the more common materials in masonry construction are brick and stone, such as marble, granite, travertine, limestone, concrete block, glass block, and tile. Masonry, when properly constructed, is very durable construction, but durability depends on materials used, workmanship, and the patterns that the units are assembled in. The strength of masonry is based on the strong and durable bonds that are formed with the masonry units of construction. Most often, masonry is used for the walls of buildings and for retaining walls. Generally, these are brick or concrete block. Rebars are used in concrete block construction to offer better tensile and lateral strength.

Veneer masonry refers to masonry units that are installed on one or both sides of a structurally independent wall made of wood or masonry. Its purpose is primarily decorative and not structural. The brick veneer is connected to the structural wall by brick ties, or metal strips that are attached to the structural wall and the brick veneer mortar joints.

Steel

Steel is an alloy consisting of mostly of iron, and a carbon content that ranges between 0.2% and 2.1% by weight. The difference in the weight of carbon changes the grade of the steel. Other alloying elements can be used, including manganese, chromium, tungsten, and vanadium. Carbon and other elements act as hardening agents. The level of alloying elements used controls the steel's hardness, ductility, and tensile strength of the final steel product. Cast iron is produced when alloys have higher carbon content than 2.1%. They also have a lower melting point and castability, hence the name cast iron. Galvanized steel uses zinc. This protects the steel against rust and corrosion.

Structural Steel is strong steel that is rolled into shapes that are used in construction. Structural steel must be fireproofed using external insulation in order to prevent the material from weakening in the event of a fire. When heated, steel expands and softens, and will lose its structural integrity. It may also melt. Fireproofing applied to steel slows the transfer of heat to the steel.

Steel is used in many different types of construction. Steel members can be used to construct the internal frame of a house using a stud framing system, where the steel resembles timber studs. Large scale construction may use trusses to increase the structural capacity of the structure. Large structures, such as industrial buildings, warehouses, recreation centers, aviation hangars and stadiums use structural steel construction. Each member is manufactured to measurement. Steel fabricators use computer modeling software to calculate the exact size and length of every piece before they are made and shipped out to site.

Steel is one of the most common materials used in large-scale bridge building. Its high-tensile capacity allows its use in the form of large steel cables in construction of suspension members and in post-tensioning systems. As previously discussed, steel is often used in conjunction with concrete in the form of reinforcement bars set inside the concrete. Concrete is a brittle material known for its compressive strength, and steel has strong tensile and ductile properties. Together, they can bear a full spectrum of forces imposed by different types of loads. Steel-reinforced concrete can be used in almost any type of structure as floor slabs, beams and columns.

Floor Systems

Floors can be built directly on a concrete slab, flat on the ground. Most flooring however is constructed raised above the ground. This is because raised flooring is more resilient, and allows for heating equipment, plumbing, electrical wiring, insulation, and other mechanical equipment running below to be accessed. The raised floor is built on a framework that acts as a bridge between one exterior wall and another. This framework, generally wood constructed, is called a joist. Wooden joists run parallel to one another at regular intervals. A similar system is used to construct a ceiling at the higher levels of a structure. In constructing a house, for example, ceilings are usually built just the way you would build a floor, except with likely lighter materials, because they are not carrying the types of loads that the flooring does. The floor joists are placed at equi-distant intervals, spanning support areas such as walls, foundations, and beams. The spacing, for example, might be 16, 12 or 24 inches "on center", which means from the center to the center. Floor joists at the foundation rests on sills that are treated so that the point of contact will not rot or be inviting to termites. Once the subfloor is constructed as the structural component, it serves as the base for finish flooring.

The Building Envelope

The building envelope separates the outside of a building from the inside. It includes walls, main floor, windows, doors, and ceilings. The envelope maintains heat and air conditioning and control moisture, and protects against the elements. The interior work of a project begins in earnest only after the envelope is completed.

Roofing System

When the architect designs a roofing system, the things that are considered and what drives the design are factors such as the design of the entire building structure, fire rating requirements, climate, loads imposed by snow, cost considerations, and the length of time of life expectancy desired. Also important is the pitch or slope of the roof. Generally roofs are pitched, meaning the angle that the roof rises from its low point to its high point. The roof system must provide proper drainage of water from roof surfaces. Very important to the performance of the roofing system is the underlayment of the roof. The roof deck must be able to properly support the application of roofing material. The roofing substrate must be smooth and free of debris.

The building "skeleton" frames the building. To complete a building's "covering" there is a stiff membrane supporting the exterior skin, and a waterproof layer of roofing material. The framing can be rafters or trusses. The decking that supports the roof can be poured or pre-cast units, wood sheathing, or concrete slabs. There is a wide range of roofing materials that are used in construction, and there are various types of roofing systems. The earliest protection against rain, heat, sunlight, cold, and wind were roofs made of straw, mud or sod over woven materials or wood. Clay tile was also used, mostly by ancient Greeks, and later on, Spaniards. Ancient Romans used slate and stone, and also copper sheeting. Asphalt was first used as a roofing material in the late 1800's. Cold tar and asphalt pitch, also called hot bitumens, are used in some roofing systems. In a shingle roof system, which most houses have, roofing felts are installed under shingles, and are called the underlayment.

You may hear architects discussing the design of a "built up" roof. This is a roof built with the alternate placement of bitumen and roofing felt, which creates a waterproof membrane, without seams. Roofing roll material that consists of felt with an asphalt coating and bituminous coating may also be used in this type of roofing system. With the sun beating down on the roof day after day, roofs endure higher temperatures that the other elements of the building, and as a result, the materials will expand and contract with heat and cold. Your designer must consider these factors in determining the roofing system. The roof slab will expand faster that any part of the building that serves as the building's structure, and allowances have to be made for this, or else the stress of the movement will cause the failure of the materials.

In a roofing system, the surface of the roof meets the vertical walls of a building. At this meeting point, *flashing* is installed to provide a water proof joint. Without flashing, water would penetrate into walls. The flashing may be plastic sheeting or sheet metal. The rainwater that collects on the roof is carried of the building with gutters, roof drains, and downspouts.

Often, a problem with roofs starts with the roof deck. Many roofing failures occur when the application is incorrect, such as applying roofing to roof decks that are not dry. The moisture that is trapped will cause blistering in the roofing materials. If the roof deck is not clean and smooth, roof coverings can be punctured. When there is a quality issue with roofs, the manufacturer of the roofing materials will be called in by the Owner or Contractor and the quality of workmanship will be carefully reviewed to determine the reasons for failure of the roofing system. This is important because there are guarantees and warranties by the manufacturer and by the Contractor, but failure to follow manufacturer's instructions becomes an issue for the Contractor, who must provide a roofing system with the proper guarantees and warranties to the Owner.

"Green" Roofs

We hear more often these days about "green roofs", usually found in LEED certified buildings (we will discuss LEED later). The market for green roofs is still young in this country. A green roof system extends an existing roofing system, providing a higher end repellant system for the natural elements, a drainage system, a filtering system, and a means to grow vegetation.

Many government entities have been working to promote green roofs and green building construction in general. There are good economic reasons to do this. Green roofs reduce runoff of storm water that would need to be treated in a municipal water treatment plant. They also protect the roof membrane from sunlight, greatly extending the life of the roof. The need not to construct a new roof every twenty years is not only a cost savings, but less material from demolition needs to be disposed into landfills. The roof is also kept cooler, and reduces cooling necessary in the summertime. Green systems may also include solar shingles that can generate electricity for hot air and hot water.

You may also see wind turbines on roofing systems to generate electricity, although there is some debate about how much electricity is really produced with the current technology.

Window System

Buildings are provided with natural light, and we achieve this through wall openings that are called windows. Usually, windows and frames are constructed of aluminum, steel and stainless steel. Wood windows cost less, but they expand and contract due to moisture. Stainless steel windows are more costly by require less maintenance and replacement. Windows are rated by the National Fenestration Rating Council. Ratings can be U-value or thermal transmittance. You will hear this term often in construction. A U-value is a measure of heat loss in a building element – a wall, floor or roof. It measures how well parts of a building can transfer heat. Therefore, the higher the U-value, the less efficient the thermal performance of the building. A lower U-value indicates that there are high levels of insulation, and less energy will be required for heating and cooling.

Windows are also rated based on their *Solar Heat Gain Coefficient*. The formulas for these values provide a decimal reading, and suffice to say that the lower the number, the better the performance of the window. Thus, an off the shelf window from Home Depot window might have a U value of .60 or a SHGC value of .60 but your Architect might specify a high performance window with a U value of .35 and a SHGG value of .4. That would be more energy efficient in maintaining heating and cooling.

Windows can be a "long lead item". Public agency administrators must be mindful that long lead items, which take time to fabricate and deliver, need to be considered in reviewing and approving a construction schedule. Other long lead items that you will encounter include but are not limited to certain types of HVAC equipment, specialty mechanical equipment, and special architectural finishes such as high end mill work.

Exterior Doors

The types of exterior doors vary but any door is hinged and swings from the door frame. Door frames include various components including side pieces called jambs and an overhead piece called a head. Hollow steel doors and frames are used frequently because they are practical. Other materials frequently used are wood, plastic, metal, glass and combinations of these materials. A door can be hollow core or solid core. In heavily traveled areas, good design calls for solid doors, due to the abuse and use they endure. Types of doors include panel doors (wood panels held in place by wood stiles and rails) and solid core doors. Wood doors may be hollow core or solid core. Solid core doors can withstand more use and abuse, and are used in more heavily traveled areas. Door types may also include panel doors, hollow metal insulated doors, and hollow core wood doors.

Local and national building codes require that certain passageways be closed with a fire door. Fire doors stop or slow the spread of a fire's path. The Underwriters Laboratories®, an independent product safety certification organization that has been testing products and writing standards for safety, provide labels that are required to be attached to the edge of the doors. Fire doors are rated A through E, and these indicate the time the door should be able to resist the spread of fire.

The Mechanical, Electrical & Plumbing (MEP) Building Systems

Once a building has been roofed and the exterior cladding has been installed, it provides sufficient protection against the elements and work can begin on the MEP systems.

The waste lines and water supply lines of the plumbing system are installed, as are fire suppression systems.

The work for heating, ventilating and air conditioning systems are carried out, including boilers, chillers, cooling towers, piping, ductwork and other components of the HVAC system.

Electrical, communications and control wiring are routed throughout the building to provide service.

Elevators and escalators are installed in structural openings provided for them.

The vertical runs of pipes, ducts and wires are made through vertical shafts that were properly sized for that purpose. Each shaft will be enclosed with fire-resistive walls to prevent the vertical spread of fire.

Horizontal runs of pipes, ducts and wired are located beneath each floor slab above the ceiling of the floor below, out of sight and out of the way. They will be accessible for maintenance and repair. Floor areas will be reserved for mechanical spaces, such as electrical distribution equipment, the boiler plant, chillers, pumps, and other heavy equipment.

In very tall buildings, an entire floor or groups of floors may be set aside for mechanical equipment, especially where the building is vertically zoned into groups of floors for service.

The roof may provide penthouses for elevator machinery and mechanical system components such as cooling towers and ventilation fans.

Plumbing

The plumbing system of a building has three main components: water supply, waste lines and vent stacks. The building water supply, waste removal and drainage systems must work independently of each other. Sewer gasses are prevented from backing up through house drains because air that enters the vent stack and vent pipes keep system traps sealed. Plumbing works with gravity.

Other natural forces in play are pressure, and the fact that water always seeks its own level. In the example of a simple residential building, there are two distinct subsystems that make up the plumbing system. One subsystem brings fresh water in and the other takes wastewater out. Water enters the building under pressure. There must be enough pressure for water to go up above the first floor level, turn corners, and go where it is needed. Meters register the amount of water use as it enters the building.

The main water shutoff valve controls the entry of water. The water will either be cold or hot. To create hot water, the piping system carries water from the cold water supply to a water heating system, and the hot water is distributed to all fixtures, outlets and appliances that need hot water. A thermostat on the heater regulates the temperature that is set.

Depending on location, a building can have a sewer system tied into a municipal sewer system or a septic system, where sewage is collected and stored for cleanout. Drainage systems, unlike water systems, do not require pressure. Drainage pipes are set at an angle or pitch, and gravity pulls the waste toward the downward pitch. The system also includes vents, traps and cleanouts. Vents are installed on roofs to allow air to enter the drainpipes so that wastewater can flow out properly. Traps are the s-curve sections of pipe under a drain. This "traps" some of the water so that a seal can be formed to prevent sewer gas from backing up into the building. All fixtures have traps, including sinks, toilets, and bathtubs.

Electrical

Electrical systems consist of three components: the service connection, including the meter and main hook-up; the breaker panel, serving as the electrical distribution center; and electrical circuits that provide the house wires that connect to every light and outlet.

Typically, electricity flows in from one of two 120 volt wires and back through a grounded neutral wire. This flow is known as "electric current". A flaw in the wire to and from these points interrupts the current's path.

The utility company will be providing electrical service to your project either through overhead or underground service lines, which feed a transformer, that functions to step down the voltage feed to the building. This is because the service coming from the utility company is at a much higher voltage than is necessary for the building's needs.

In the simple residential building construction we described earlier, the utility company provided power to the house meter using two 120 volt wires and a grounded neutral wire. The meter is a watt measuring device supplied by the utility company to track each month's power consumption. There are meters with numbered dials like a watch on older models and new state-of-the-art digital meters that can be read right from the utility company's office. The electrical panel, breaker box, fuse box or service panel (it is known by many names) is the next device in line. This panel's job is to distribute power throughout your home and disconnect power from the incoming feed. The power (electrical distribution from the utility company) comes in to a main breaker and is usually 100 or 200 amps. Individual breakers then distribute individual circuits (called branch circuits) throughout a typical house. In this example, the breakers range in size from 15 to 100 amps. Lighting circuits would be 15 amps, outlet circuits would be 20 amps, and a sub panel circuit to a garage or tool shed would usually be 60 or 100 amps.

In the design phase of the public project, the electrical engineer will specify service and distribution of electricity as required by the building program developed by the Architect. The power system is generally considered to be a combination of two sections: the transmission and the distribution. The difference between the two sections depends on the function of each at that particular time. At times, in a small power system, the difference tends to disappear, and the transmission section merges with the distribution section. The delivery network, as a whole, is referred to as the distribution section and is normally used to designate the outside lines and frequently continues inside the building to include power outlets.

Most building facilities use *alternating current* (AC), not *direct current*

(DC). This is because transformers can only be used with AC. Alternators, or generators, a wiring system of feeders that carry generated power to a distribution center, and the distribution center itself, which distributes power to wiring systems called primary and secondary mains constitute most land based power systems.

Electrical current is commonly measured in watts, amps and volts. The voltage is analogous to water pressure; it measures the "pressure" of the electricity being "pushed" through the wire. Wattage is the quantity of electricity being pushed through the wire. Amperage is the result of wattage divided by voltage. So if you see a device rated for "15 amps", that means when supplied with 120 volt current, it is designed to handle up to 1800 watts (15 amps x 120 volts = 1800 watts).

A *panel board* is a component of the electrical supply system that divides an electrical power feed into subsidiary circuits while providing a protective circuit breaker or fuse in each circuit that will cut off power in the circuit if it demands causes a power overload.

Circuit breakers and fuses are important safety devices. They work effectively as a switch and are designed to stop the flow of electricity. While a circuit breaker is very much like a switch, fuses have a one time usage and must be replaced each time they protect a circuit. When too much load is placed on a circuit, the breaker "trips" and interrupts the flow of electricity.

An excessive load may result from too many devices simultaneously in use on a circuit, a faulty device or a short circuit, amongst other possibilities. Without a circuit breaker, an overloaded device could be damaged; a fire could result from the heat generated by the device or wiring or from electrical sparking. Circuit breakers however are not very effective at protecting people from electrocution. The problem is that they do not trip quickly enough to protect you from harm. That is why most electrical codes now call for Ground Fault Circuit Interrupters ("GFCI"), often located in wet locations such as kitchens and bathrooms. It is an inexpensive electrical device that, if installed in household branch circuits, shuts off power if there is excessive current flowing.

HVAC

HVAC is an acronym for "Heating, Ventilation and Air Conditioning" systems. The HVAC system controls the temperature and the air quality in the conditioned space. The technology for this system is based on thermodynamics, fluid mechanics and the transfer of heat. HVAC system design is considered to be part of the discipline of mechanical engineering. As you might imagine, HVAC is critical in the design of large facilities and multiple story buildings, where a healthy building relies on the proper regulation of humidity and temperature, and the supply of fresh air from outside.

Heating
Various types of heating systems are designed based on the requirements of the building and its function. Central heating is generally used in cold climates for private housing and public buildings. The system's components include the boiler, furnace, or heat pump for the heating of water, steam or air in a central location, such as the mechanical room in a large facility. When water is used as the method to transfer heat, the system is known as hydronics.

The system will distribute heat via ductwork for forced air systems or piping for the distribution of the heated fluid, and radiators to transfer this heat to the air. This is done through the process known as convection. In a system that uses radiators, these devices are mounted on walls or buried in floors. The boiler fed heating system uses pumps to circulate the water to ensure that heat is supplied equitably to all of the radiators. The heated water may also be fed through a heat exchanger and storage tank to provide hot running water.

Heat is distributed through ductwork in the forced air system. This system can also be adapted for air conditioning. Heating is also provided from an electric filament that heats up, and is typical of baseboard and portable electric heating. It is also used as a back up for a heat pump when temperatures are extreme.

Ventilation

A space is ventilated by replacing air in a given space for the purpose of controlling temperature, removing moisture, dust, smoke, carbon dioxide and other substances, and to provide oxygen. The systems installed include the exchange of air to the outside, and the circulation of inside air within the building. Ventilation can be natural ventilation or forced or mechanical ventilation. An example of a mechanical or forced ventilation system is the exhaust in your kitchen. The design of the appropriate system by your designer must take into account such factors as noise and required flow rates.

Natural ventilation is simply the ventilation of a facility using outside air without resorting to mechanical systems. It is achieved through operable windows and vents installed in the building envelope.

Cooling

Air conditioning systems are based on the removal of warm air and its recycling back as cool air. The cycle continues until the desired temperature is achieved. Acting much like a refrigerator without an insulated box, the system uses the evaporation of a refrigerant to provide cooling. In a simple air conditioning system, the compressor compresses the refrigerant so that it becomes hot, high pressure gas. The gas runs through a set of coils so that its heat is dissipated, and condenses to a liquid. The refrigerant liquid runs through an expansion valve, and during this process it evaporates to become a cold gas. The cold gas runs through a set of coils, and the gas absorbs heat and cools down the air inside the space being cooled. While the above system basically describes a window air conditioner that would cool a relatively small space, there will be larger, more efficient systems required for your building project.

One such system is called the "split" system. A split-system air conditioner splits the hot side from the cold side of the system. The cold side is simply the expansion valve and the cold coil, placed in an air handler. The air handler blows air through the coil, and the air is directed through the building with ductwork. The hot side, or the condensing unit, is outside of the building. The unit contains a spiral coil, a fan to blow air through the coil, and a weather resistant compressor. In large facilities, you will find the condensing unit on the roof, and may be very large, or many smaller units, each attached to an air handler that cools a specific zone in the building.

In very large buildings, the split system is not feasible, because the runs of piping needed between the condenser and air handler are too long to function correctly. In this case, a chilled water system may be used. With this system, you will find the entire air conditioner on the roof or behind the building. It will cool water to between 40 and 45 degrees Fahrenheit, and the chilled water is piped into the building and distributed to air handlers. With a well insulated chilled water pipe, length of the pipe is not an issue and therefore this system makes sense. Each system used uses air to dissipate heat from the outside coil.

In large systems, a cooling tower makes the system more efficient by creating a stream of lower temperature water that runs through a heat exchanger, and cools the hot coils of the air conditioner unit. Although expensive compared to other systems, its payback in energy savings over time allows the system to pay for itself. Cooling towers all work the same way, regardless of shape and size.

The cooling tower blows air through the stream of water, causing some of the water to evaporate. The water trickles through an open plastic mesh sheet, and air blows through it. The evaporation cools the water stream. As water is lost from its evaporation, the cooling tower adds more water to make up the difference. In many office complexes and college campuses, cooling towers and air conditioning equipment are centralized, and chilled water is routed to all of the buildings through a distribution system consisting of miles of underground pipes.

Highway and Roadway Construction

Construction operations for highway and roadways include new construction of highways and bridges and the rehabilitation of existing highway, roadway and bridge infrastructure. Work may include: (a). Preventative maintenance; (b). Repair, repave or reconstruct with or without bridges; and (c). New construction.

New construction of a typical four lane highway will involve the following construction processes:
- Topographic, right-of-way and utility Surveys
- Utility relocations
- Environmental mitigation
- Bridge construction
- Grading and paving
- Lighting and signing

Once the land has been acquired and a Contractor retained through a public process, construction work begins at the site of the new highway. Construction signs are installed to warn motorists of the work. Any utilities that may be affected are removed and/or relocated. Environmental measures such as silt fences and erosion control structures are installed around any watercourses.

The area where the road is to be built is cleared of trees, some of which may be salvaged. After the trees have been removed, the remaining stumps are removed by equipment with root rakes, which do not remove the valuable topsoil.

Most roads are designed to maximize the material available on site. This is called common excavation or solid rock excavation. Excavated material is moved by large equipment such as bulldozers, excavators, and trucks. However, sometimes some material needs to be imported to the site. This material is referred to as the "borrow".

As the highway is constructed, layers of soil, rock and crushed rock are compacted by equipment to make the road strong. As work continues, exposed areas are stabilized by planting grass. Areas that are prone to erosion are protected by rock called riprap. The final grading involves the placement of topsoil on the slopes and to hydroseed it to plant grass. Now, the road is ready for paving with asphalt.

Structures are used to carry traffic over other roads, railway tracks, or water. Structures are also called overpasses, underpasses, or bridges. Structures can be single span or multi-span with columns between each span. A structure consists of footings, piers, pier caps, abutments, beams and a deck. The footing is the base of the structure. The pier sits on top of the footing and supports the pier cap. The pier cap supports the beams and the beams in turn support the deck. The abutments form the start and end of the structure and support the beams as well.

The first step in building a structure is to build a strong footing. Generally the structure is located on ground that will properly support it. If required, piles are driven to provide the necessary support. Once this is done, the shape of the footing is determined using a "form" and concrete is poured into the form. Once the footing is hard enough, piers are "formed" on top, followed by the pier cap. The abutments are then completed. Once all of this work is complete, beams are placed. Beams can be either concrete or steel. Once the beams are placed, then the deck is placed. A protective barrier wall is installed and the deck is waterproofed to prevent water from seeping into the concrete. This is followed by the paving of the deck with asphalt, and pavement marking to delineate travel lanes.

Generally, asphalt is used to pave highways and roadways, as well as city streets and parking lot areas. Asphalt is a flexible material that is bitumen naturally formed or the product of petroleum refining. Asphalt is a mixture of stone, sand and asphalt cement, which gives the asphalt its black look and binds everything together. A key quality issue in the use of asphalt is plant mixing. Stationary mixing plants provide large quantities of high quality, hot mixtures for application. They are made at batch type plans or drum mix plants. Each processes the aggregate that is included in the mix differently.

Asphalt concrete is a combination of aggregate that is mixed hot with paving asphalt at a control plant. The mix must meet ASTM specifications for construction materials. Hot mix material is transported to the job site in dump trucks and placed with mechanical spreaders to a specified thickness. A sub base installation involves the placement of materials that will improve the foundation for the surfacing of the site. These are constructed with materials that compact well to provide continuous and uniform underlying support. It must have sufficient bearing strength to carry the load that will travel on the paved surface. The surfacing asphalt is placed and compacted to provide a smooth and dense surface for traffic to drive on. It is sloped so that the water rolls off the highway. Once the asphalt has been placed, the guide rail is installed, electrical wiring is run to provide power to the lights, and signs are installed.

Chapter 2 References

The following sources were utilized in writing this chapter:

Allen, E. and Iano, J. Fundamentals of Building Construction. Materials and Methods. 4th Edition. John Wiley and Sons, Inc. 2004. Hoboken NJ

Watson, D. Construction Materials and Processes. 3rd Edition. McGraw-Hill, Inc. 1986. New York, NY

Holtz, R. and Kovacs, W. (1981), *An Introduction to Geotechnical Engineering*, Prentice-Hall, Inc

American Concrete Institute. www.concrete.org

American Iron and Steel Institute. www.steel.org

Chapter 3
Procurement of Professional Services

Roles of the Agency's Project Design and Construction Management Project Team

The Architect

The Architect is a licensed design professional who assists in the programming, planning, and development of designs, drawings, specifications and other technical submissions, at various stages of development during the design phase. An agency may also pay the Architect for services rendered during the bid and award and construction phases of the project. These services will include responding to questions from bidders and issuing clarifications during bid and award, and during the construction of the project, reviews and approvals of shop drawings and submittals provided by the Contractor, performing construction site observations, and responding to requests for clarifications and working on field change designs. Large public projects usually require the retention of a Construction Manager or Resident Engineer to manage the day to day operations, and rely on the Architect for non-supervisory services during construction.

In most cases, unless the project is driven by engineering disciplines, the Agency will issue the RFP to the Architect as the prime consultant, and the Architect will assemble a team that includes, as requires, land surveyors, landscape architects, geotechnical engineers, civil Engineers, structural engineers, mechanical, electrical and plumbing (MEP) engineers and other specialty consultants, and is responsible for the co-ordination of the technical services of these other parties and integration of their design elements into the construction contract documents.

The Architect assists the agency by developing program requirements for the building. The objective initially is to formulate a design concept that meets the requirements of the users of the facility. This involves a series of meetings with the Agency and the users of the facility in order to collect data sufficient to determine the requirements of the client. The development of a palpable program is critical to the design effort. The architect selected for the project needs to have a familiarity with local regulations and building codes, and applicable state and federal codes and regulations. At the local level, the architect needs to understand and meet compliance requirements for planning and zoning laws which govern building setbacks, heights of buildings, parking capacity requirements, applicable historic preservations requirements, special requirements like art commission compliance, etc.

The Architect is the agent of the Owner / Agency. The Agency is selecting a particular architect based on the belief that the architect is fully qualified and capable of providing the best possible design considering the constraints of time, money, practicality, and feasibility. The Agency is transferring the complete responsibility of the design to the Architect, and is therefore obligated to provide the Architect with all the resources and information it has at its disposal and to ensure cooperation of the user group whose input and cooperation the Architect requires to complete the program and the design. All program objectives must be clearly conveyed to the Architect. It is important to note that even if an agency employs its own architects and engineers to review submissions by the contracted architect, this in no way relieves the Architect of responsibilities to provide competent, code compliant design, nor does it relieve the architect from liability that is the consequences of faulty design under errors and omission clauses of the consulting contract with the Architect.

The Architect will have the primary responsibility of producing and coordinating the plans and specifications. This requires that the Architect provide plans and specifications in sufficient detail to convey with accuracy the complete project in a manner that will allow it to be built as designed and specified.

The Architect should not seek to transfer any design risk to other members of the project team. Nothing in the drawings and specifications pertinent to design, for example, should be shifted to the Contractor. This means that each building component must be sufficiently detailed and described in a manner that allows for that component to be built specifically as designed by the Architect. Thus, in every aspect, the construction contract documents should be technically correct. For example, specified equipment must be properly located and is provided with adequate electrical service to power it. The responsibility for coordinating design issues belongs to the Architect and not the Contractor or the Construction Manager.

The design presented to the Agency must be workable and buildable. If the pieces do not fit, you can expect a change order or a claim from your Contractor in the construction phase. When bidding, some contracts will bid knowing that the design documents are deficient, and will plan for claims later on by stating that additional work was required above the bid requirements. Everything needs to work properly. Electrical service needs to be adequate, the HVAC system needs to be properly sized, every pipe diameter needs to be adequate for conveyance.

As the project progresses to construction, there will be a need to interpret aspects of the construction contract documents. The Architect's role will be to interpret the documents to either provide clarification or to assist in resolving a dispute. As these questions arise, it is usually because of inconsistency, questions of the designer's intent, or an incomplete design. However, it can also be motivated by the fact that the Contractor did not price this aspect of the work to his satisfaction, and is raising questions as a prelude to a claim or change request for out of scope work or unforeseen field conditions.

It is important that the Architect provide a prompt response for shop drawings and other submittals from the Contractor. This is a time consuming process, but the Agency needs to be assured that there is a system in place for the Architect to receive, review and return submittals with approval recommendations in a timely fashion. The Agency's Construction Manager may be monitoring this process. The contract documents should be clear about the submittal process and the requirements of all parties in this endeavor. The Architect will review shop drawings to determine that these submissions are in compliance with the contract. The submissions will also be reviewed for completeness by the Contractor. Other reviews by the Architect during construction include:

- Review and recommendations for change orders and the preparation of design for changes in the work
- Approval of payment applications
- Issuance of meeting minutes for design issues
- On site investigations and inspections as provided in the contract, as applicable
- Monitoring acceptability of materials and workmanship
- Preparing clarifications and respond to on-going questions
- Investigating existing field conditions that have not been addressed in the documents
- Evaluating work in place and determine acceptability
- Determining dates of substantial completion

The specific role of the Architect in the construction phase varies, and it is important for the Agency to clearly specify exactly what is required if the Architect in this phase. All too frequently, public RFPs understate the role expected of the Architect, and scopes of service that require "periodic" spot inspections and reviews morph into demands for more frequent services. The Agency needs to consider compensating the Architect on a time and material basis where the role of an architect is expanded beyond the original intent of the contract. This is also true for meetings at the job site.

Generally, the Architect's role in construction is greater for smaller projects that may not have a Construction Manager. In these cases, the Architect may be providing full services including daily inspection of work, review and approval of payment requisitions, and other functions.

On larger scale projects, an independent Construction Manager will provide daily inspection of work and coordinate all construction phase activities, working cooperatively with the Architect as a resource as required.

The American Institute of Architects (AIA) provides titles and job descriptions for architectural firms. The senior principal or partner may an equity position in the firm, is the signatory to the contract and is ultimately responsible for performance. Partners are generally senior vice presidents or vice presidents. Depending on the size of the firm, there are department heads, senior managers, Project Managers, licensed architects at various levels, and designers and drafters who may have a degree in architecture but may not be licensed.

The Engineer

If the Agency is engaged in heavy civil works, such as transportation, rail, waste water treatment, water supply, and utilities, the primary design lead may be the Engineer, and not the Architect. Much of what has been said about the role of the Architectural firm applies to the Engineer when the Engineer leads the team. In turn, the Engineer may retain the Architect as a sub consultant or joint venture partner, depending on the scope and level of architectural services required.

The Engineer is a professional who is licensed by the state to provide professional engineering services in the state where the engineer practices. There are various engineering disciplines that will be involved in your project.

Civil Engineers are qualified to design, construct and maintain public works, including roads, bridges, sanitary and water supply facilities, rail facilities, highways and expressways, harbors, etc. They are also engaged to provide site and utility design for building projects. There are sub-disciplines of civil engineering. These include: environmental engineering, geotechnical engineering, structural engineering, transportation engineering, water resources engineering, sanitary engineering, material engineering, land surveying, and construction engineering.

The focus of civil engineering is on the surface features of a project. They specialize in site development, drainage, pavement; water supply, sanitary systems, site utilities that convey electrical and communications. Civil Engineers provide engineering and design services that convert land from one usage to another. To accomplish this, the engineering sub-divisions mentioned above are incorporated by the civil engineer. Civil engineers are also engaged in water resources and management. This discipline includes hydrology, environmental science, conservation, and geology.

Geotechnical Engineering focuses on earth materials, using principles of soil mechanics to investigate subsurface conditions and materials to determine the suitability of subsurface conditions to support the construction of a project at the site. Subsurface conditions may include natural rock and soil conditions, chemical properties of existing materials, materials that exist as a result of previous construction or man made deposits at the site, the stability of natural slopes. The services provided by geotechnical engineers are critical to the design of foundations, and the overall suitability of the site to support the project structure. The geotechnical engineer is typically engaged by the Architect or Engineer of record to investigate soil conditions by performing or supervising the taking of borings for soil samples that are analyzed in a laboratory. A geotechnical report of findings discusses the suitability of these materials to support construction. The geotechnical engineer identifies and designs the type of foundation or earthwork required to support the structures to be built.

Structural Engineers provide for the structural analysis and structural design of buildings, bridges, and other structures. They determine loads that will act on the structure and the forces and stresses that the structure will have based on those loads. Loads are described as dead loads and live loads. Dead loads include the weight of the structure itself, and other dead load, and live loads are created by moving load (trucks and automobiles, people) wind load, earthquake load, load from temperature change etc. The structural engineer must design structures to be safe for their users and to allow the structure to function as intended by the design. Seismic design requirements are now imposed by local building codes to deal with earthquake loads. Structural design will consider strength, stiffness, and the stability of the structure, and the ability to support self-weight, wind, seismic, crowd or vehicle loads.

Land surveying involves the measurement of dimensions in the surface of the earth. Surveyors use equipment including levels and theodolites to measure horizontal and vertical and slope distances. Other equipment used by surveyors includes electronic distance measurement, total stations, Global Position Stationing (GPS), and laser scanning. Civil engineers learn the basics of land surveying when they are being trained as engineers. Land surveying is considered to be a distinct discipline, and land surveyors are licensed in the state where they perform land surveying services. Typically, the survey crew consists of the party chief, who may or may not be licensed, an instrument person, and sometimes, a rod person. They work under the supervision of a licensed land surveyor who will seal and certify the survey. Surveyors are engaged to assist in the lay out of routes for transportation systems, roads, and utilities.

Another branch of surveying is **construction surveying**. These technicians survey existing conditions of the work site, including topography, existing buildings and infrastructure. They lay out or stake out reference points to guide new construction of roads, buildings and other construction. They verify the location of structures during the construction process. They will also provide as-built surveying when the project ends to verify that the work was completed in accordance with the plans.

Transportation Engineering involves designing and constructing transportation infrastructure. These include city streets, highways, rail systems, canals, airports, bridges, ports, and mass transit. The services provided include transportation design, transportation planning, traffic engineering, Intelligent Transportation Systems (ITS), signalization, and the management of infrastructure.

Mechanical Engineers are licensed to provide for the design and construction of building systems that include central plant heating and cooling systems, including boiler and chiller design, cooling tower design, cooling tower design, pumping systems, heating water, chilled water and condensers, office VAV systems, water piping systems, and other systems typical to the type of facility being constructed.

Electrical Engineers are licensed to provide electrical systems and electrical sub-systems required for the services required by the facility. These include electrical service, lighting design, fire alarm design and layout, telecommunications systems, computer room UPS design, public address systems, and security system infrastructure design.

Plumbing Engineers are licensed to provide a variety of plumbing design systems that include waste and vent systems, domestic water and hot water systems, central domestic water heating, storm water systems, plumbing systems, grease waste systems, sump pump and sewage ejector systems, medical gas systems for hospitals, natural gas piping systems, and high pressure process piping systems.

The Construction Manager and Resident Engineer

Many public agencies refer to the term "Construction Manager" for the firm that is hired to manage and supervise the construction of buildings and facilities. Transportation agencies typically require the management of their projects in construction to be performed by a firm that is licensed to provide professional engineering services, and the manager of construction is often referred to as the "Resident Engineer". Typically the Resident Engineer supervises the construction of heavy civil infrastructure, including bridges, highways, water supply, sanitary and rail. There are no hard and fast rules and these terms have been interchanged by different agencies. Each agency determines how it uses the Construction Manager and Resident Engineering terms.

There are two basic forms of Construction Management (CM) delivery, with variations. These are: Agency CM and CM-at-Risk or Guaranteed Maximum Price (GMP) CM. The Agency will likely want to procure the services of a CM when the project is complex, and/or where budget, time and quality are key concerns driving the project. Many agency contracts with the CM provide for the Agency CM to manage the work of the Architect and the construction Contractor. Other arrangements do not provide CM control over the Architect, and the CM may hold the contracts for the Contractor directly as agent, or the Agency itself will directly contract with Contractors.

There is another layer of bureaucracy on projects where the CM is engaged. This is appropriate especially where the Agency does not have the expertise or resources to manage the project, and therefore relies on the CM firm for this. CM firms will often state at presentations to the Agency that they are "an extension" of the Owner.

Depending on the size of the project and its complexity, the staffing of the project by the CM will vary. The author, as a construction management consultant, has staffed several projects as Agency CM to public agencies for projects up to $60 million with four personnel: a Project Manager, office engineer, General Superintendent, and mechanical/electrical/plumbing (MEP) inspector. Larger and more complex projects require more staffing. A project may have, in addition to the named positions, additional Superintendents and inspectors, a site safety manager, a project engineer, scheduler, cost engineer, a contract administrator, and clerical support personnel.

The CM Project Manager (PM) is the person that is in charge of the complete execution of the construction project. This position reports to a higher level of authority within the CM firm, usually a project executive who is not full time on the project, or a senior vice president of operations. The CM Project Manager is usually a full time position. This position is the focal point of the construction project, interacting with the Owner / agency, facility managers, Architect and Engineer, trade Contractors, unions, vendors and other parties. The Project Manager oversees all jobsite functions, and marshals all required corporate resources required from the home office of the CM. The PM organizes and manages procurement, field supervision and quality assurance, monitoring of contractor safety programs and compliance, progress schedules, coordination issues, claims and change order reviews, payment requisitions, maintaining communication with correspondence, emails, minutes of progress and job meetings, and the project closeout. This includes obtaining contractor guarantees, manufacturer warranties, training of maintenance staff in the operation of new equipment, and the final turnover of the facility.

The Superintendent on a building project supervises all field activities. On a large project, a General Superintendent may have overall responsibility, with other Superintendents reporting to this position. It is the role of the Superintendent to ensure that the contractor has adequate staffing and equipment, and competent subcontractors at the site. The position requires the ability to plan in advance to assure that materials and equipment, and manpower are available when required to progress the work. This includes the ability to identify field construction and work sequences and monitoring performance within accepted industry practice for construction and compliance with the plans and specifications of the construction contract documents.

On heavy construction projects, or resident engineering contracts, the General Superintendent's counterpart is the Chief Inspector or Assistant Resident Engineer, who supervises, in turn, senior inspectors and inspectors for the construction of roads, utilities, highways and bridges, and other heavy civil projects. The Agency may require that inspectors have certain qualifications, including engineering degrees, NICET Certification, ACI certification, and other special certifications. NICET refers to National Institute for Certification in Engineering Technologies and is granted through requisite experience at different levels and testing. ACI refers to the

American Concrete Institute, which certifies inspectors in material testing and quality for concrete. Other certifications include Asphalt Technician Certification, for inspection of highway paving, and the National Association of Corrosion Engineers (NACE), for the inspection of bridge and steel painting and coating operations.

Just as the Superintendent administers to the field, the Project Engineer administers to the office. This position coordinates the complete construction and administration of the various bid packages, and organizes the office management systems needed to establish, monitor and follow-up on the requirements of the contractor and compliance issues.

For heavy civil projects, the counterpart position is likely to be the Office Engineer, reporting to the Resident Engineer and providing many similar functions. In building projects, particularly a large complex project, the office engineer may report to the Project Engineer and carry out the detailed daily functions involving submittals, contract issues, correspondence, requisitions and other functions.

The Cost Engineer or project accountant position oversees financial management. On smaller projects, this function may be performed by the Project Engineer or Office Engineer. The function includes the establishment of all files related to contract, billing, payroll, labor and material costs. Job cost information is maintained on a current basis, and cost management reports are prepared to track expenditures against the budget. This position also provides information concerning compliance with equal employment opportunity (EEO) requirements and the utilization of minority business enterprises (MBE), woman owned business enterprises (WBE), small business enterprises (SBE), etc.

The project scheduler may be a field position, depending on the size and complexity of the project, or an office support position. This position takes the lead in the development of the project schedule, and assesses performance and compliance with the schedule. The schedule is usually prepared using software such as Primavera P3 and P6. The position evaluates and reports on project progress by the contractor, regular CPM schedule analysis, reviews of baseline and progress schedules, and participates in processes leading to the mitigation of project schedule delays. Schedulers are also utilize to review the schedule with respect to construction claims, analyzing manpower and cost loading factors.

Developing the Request for Proposal (RFP)

The RFP

The Agency seeks outside consultants when it doesn't have sufficient in house expertise or personnel available to directly provide design or construction management services.

A **request for proposal (RFP)** is prepared at an early stage of a project. RFPs by public agencies are typically issued to the Architect / Engineer and the Construction Manager. The RFP is written so that the Agency can make a determination of the best qualified firm to provide its services on your project. The Agency's RFPs should be formatted so that all respondents provide their responses in a structured and uniformly formatted way, so that the reviewers and the selection panel convened for this process can review each proposal in a way often referred to as "apples to apples", meaning that the review is of similarly formatted documents containing all required content. The RFP should be structured so that it is easy for evaluators to assess responses and rate responders in accordance to the selection criteria established for the solicitation. It is therefore important that proposals that are received address all aspects of the proposal that they will be rated on.

Request for Quotation (RFQ)

A request for quotation (RFQ) is sometimes used when a formal RFP is not necessary because specifications of products or services are already known, or if the bidders have already been prequalified through a term or requirements contract. Here, the only real consideration is price. An RFQ might also be used in order to determine price ranges before the actual RFP is issued.

Invitation for Bid (IFB)

The Invitation for Bid is used by certain agencies when the primary consideration is the lowest price to make the award. Bidders have already been pre-qualified for the work, so the selection is price driven.

When to Use the RFP Process

A request for qualifications (RFQ) is used before the RFP is issued, in order to gather information on prospective bidders and generate a pool of qualified bidders. In this process, a short list of bidders may be selected based on the review of their qualifications, and RFPs will only be issued to this pool. The RFP is written when the Agency has defined a need and is requesting consultants to propose the best method to assist the Agency in meeting the need. The submitted RFP will describe the consultant's skills, expertise and technical capability of the respondents. The Agency will evaluate the response in selecting the best qualified respondent.

Price should not be the primary or only consideration in selecting a consultant. The quality of the consultant's technical response, its proposed management and professional team member's qualifications and experience, and other factors are evaluated in determining the winning proposal.

Formatting the RFP

The RFP should be organized and clearly written. Sentences should be relatively short, and if there are numerous points to make, a vertical list is easier to follow. This allows for the highlighting of important topics and helps the reader to understand the order in which things happen, and the order of response. It also helps the reader to identify the steps that must be followed in the process RFPs issued by public agencies are typically formatted to provide for the following:

- Introduction and overview
- Background information for the project
- Scope of work
- Contract term of performance
- Definition of terms

Introduction and Overview
This section should identify the name of the project and other

identifying information. The statute that authorizes the procurement can be stated. The project should be briefly described. The objectives of the RFP and services sought should be stated.

Background

This section is a brief narrative providing background information about the project. For example, it may begin with a description of the site or facility where the work is to be performed. This should include a description of the functions and operations that will take place in the completed facility or other pertinent information that allows the proposer to have insight and to show how the firm's experience on other projects may be relevant to this one.

Scope of Work

A clearly defined scope of work should be presented so that the bidder will be able to provide a comprehensive technical approach to performing these services, and can take into account the level of effort that will be required to adequately price the proposal. This section is the core of the RFP. It outlines in detail what the Agency requires respondents to include in the proposal in response to the RFP.

Project Timetable

The entire project timeline should be included in this section. Also included should be a schedule of the RFP process (i.e. Pre-Proposal Conference, Deadlines, and Opening Date).

Pre-Proposal Conference

The RFP should announce the opportunity for bidders to meet in a Pre-proposal Conference hosted by the Agency or its agent. Pre-proposal conferences are not always necessary or required by the Agency. However, pre-proposal conferences have certain advantages:

- They allow the bidders to obtain information and insights that may not be specifically conveyed in the RFP. During this session, it allows prime consultants (those who are bidding to hold the prime contract) and prospective subconsultants and contractors to attend, learn about the project, and ask questions that all bidders can hear answers to.

- It can also be a forum for MBE, WBE and DBE firms to attend, learn who the bidders are, and offer services for prime bidders to meet goals that may be in place for the utilization of these firms. Other specialty contractors and consultant may also attend for the same reason, or are already part of a bidding team.
- If a pre-proposal conference is mandatory, then proposers who did not attend are ineligible to submit a proposal, and the RFP should state that: *"Failure to attend the pre-proposal conference will result in disqualification of the respondent's proposal."*
- The conference covers information in the solicitation document and requirements, and the agenda. There may also be a site visit that is arranged for responders. There must be a sign in sheet for attendees.
- Opening remarks at the conference should include the purpose of the conference, the project name and the solicitation number, and a review of the pertinent parts of the RFP document.
- All agency representatives that are present should be introduced. Any significant developments or addendum should be discussed.
- It is important to state that oral statements in the conference are not binding. Only written responses to questions will be valid and will be distributed to attendees, likely in the form of an addendum.

Attendees usually want copies of sign in sheets. Some agencies do not want to provide these for some reason or other, but the attendance sheets are in fact helpful to MBE and WBE firms, other subcontractors and prime consultants that are still forming teams, or want to know who they are bidding against. However, it is up to the Agency to determine the policy for this.

Technical Proposal

The technical proposal will be divided into sections. It could be formatted as described below.

A. Proposer Information
This section contains information for proposers that is needed in order to prepare the proposal in a responsive way. Topics that are included in this section include: (a). Key dates for proposal submittal; (b). Proposal compliance information including documents that must be submitted with the proposal response, the manner of response and how each is to be submitted (e.g. technical proposal, fee proposal). If the fee proposal must be separated from the technical proposal and separately sealed, this should be stated; (c). Contact information for the proposer should be submitted, such as the lead firm and contact person, licensing and certification information, and telephone, fax, email addresses and the street address of the proposer. Other information might include the MBE/WBE/DBE status of a firm, the type of work or specialty and size of firm; and the requirement for the signature of the lead individual, and the date of the signature.

B. Experience and Personnel
This section provides for the experience of the firm and key personnel resumes for evaluation. The project descriptions and resumes should clearly show the relevancy of project and staff experience for this engagement. The parts of this section may include requirements to provide a description of (a). The history of the firm's experience providing the professional services being solicited, including projects performed for government entities and authorities, private developers, and other clients; (b). The identification of experience related to the design (if an architect) or construction management (if a CM) of a retrofit, rehabilitation or new facility construction, as applicable, and specialty construction items that will be part of the advertised project.; (c) A description and organization chart of the firm's structure describing the responsibilities of the staff to be assigned to the project, including

resumes of the principals, Project Manager(s), and professional staff who would work directly with the Agency; (d). A requirement to disclose comparable projects that the firm has completed in the areas of architecture, engineering and/or construction management as Agency or Design –Built / GMP, including the names of the client, the name of a contact person who is able to provide a reference, a description of the scope and nature of the work, the size and complexity of the project, and the dollar amount and the agreed fee arrangements. State outcomes of project- awards, technical issues, significant issues, etc. It is also important to have the proposer identify their specific role on the project, such as prime consultant, joint venture partner or subconsultant; (e). Any other information that the Agency should be aware of for consideration of the firm for selection.

C. Methodology / Approach to the Project
The narrative description prepared by the proposer should demonstrate an understanding of the project requirements and the approach proposed to execute the work. Originality rather than boiler plate responses, and a direct link of approach to the specifics of the project are desirable. The respondent should be required to explain how the consultant intends to address the anticipated scope of services set forth in the RFP. This requires a statement explaining the firm's approach to the project, and how it intends to provide the services that the Agency requires in a way that meets the Agency's needs. The Agency will read all of the proposals and determine which respondent has the best approach, and this is one of the most important criteria for selection of the consultant for the Agency's project. Reviewers can determine if the approach is practical and demonstrates an understanding of the project's challenges, and the resourcefulness and experience of the proposer in the way this response is prepared. This section of the proposal should provide the respondents with an opportunity to demonstrate innovative and creative approaches to the project for save, timely and cost effective completion of the project.

D. Current Workload and Conflicts of Interest. In this section, the respondent provides a *statement of its current workload* and other outside commitments. This is important because the respondent needs to demonstrate that they have the staff, resources and capacity to complete this project as well as work that they are performing for others that may be happening around the same time that services will be required for the Agency. The proposer must assure that it can provide the necessary executive skills, staff manpower and resources to achieve the goals and timetable for this project. The proposer must also submit a statement describing any potential conflict of interest that could be created by providing services under this contract, and indicate of there is any pending litigation and/or regulatory action by any oversight body or entity that could have an adverse material impact on the firm's ability to serve. The respondent also needs to disclose whether it has been terminated from a project for any reason, and explain why the contract was terminated.

E. *Non-discrimination Policy*

- Submission of the offeror's EEO Statement and Affirmative Action Plan
- Statement of commitment to equal opportunity and affirmative action from the chief executive officer.
- Projected workforce utilization forms indicating utilization of female and minority group members.

F. Delivery of Proposals

This section outlines acceptable methods of delivery (i.e. U.S. Postal Service, Hand Delivery or Express Mail). The address to which the RFP must be delivered in order to be considered responsive is included in this section.

G. Proposal Opening

The date, time, and location that the RFP will open should be listed in this section, if there is in fact a public proposal opening...

H. Proposal Evaluation and Award

This section should describe how the proposal will be evaluated for consideration as the selected consulting firm for this project. This may include a list of specific criteria and scoring methodologies.

Cost Proposal Requirements/Content

Fee proposal requirements should be structured and formatted by the Agency, so that all bidders respond in the same format for each required scope or work or service.

Architectural and Engineering Fees:
Public agencies frequently pay design fees through a negotiated fixed price type contract. There can be other forms of cost proposals and contracts used. For example, a cost plus type contract might be used if the scope of services is not clearly defined, and the consultant will be paid on a time and material basis. Fees are also sometimes negotiated as a percentage of the construction cost. The fee presented in a cost proposal for professional services is based on three factors: direct labor costs, overhead costs, and proposed profit. The cost for reimbursable expenses incurred for working on the project should be reimbursed "dollar for dollar" with no markup.

The Architect / Engineer, preparing a fee for the fixed price contract, should be required to break his costs down for each category of service. Within each category, the classifications of professionals to be used, the estimated hours for the task, the direct hourly rate paid to staff, and the overhead and profit markups should be indicated. The cost of additional consultants is also included. The hourly rates tabulated on the form should be backed up with certified payroll records. The cost of principals and partners are usually compensated at a direct billing rate.

Reimbursable Items: Items for which the A/E will be reimbursed for "Out-of-pocket" expenses and that may not be included in the fee proposal are professional services such as site survey, sub-surface investigations, etc., reproduction of contract drawings and specifications, mylars for record (as-built) drawings, amendments and shop drawings, and mailing cost of bidding documents and amendments.

Overhead: Overhead generally refers to allowable indirect costs which cannot be directly allocated to the work although essential to the performance thereof. The method of allocating overhead costs must be in accordance with generally accepted accounting procedures. Detailed criteria for the inclusion or exclusion of components of overhead should be referenced in the contract documents that are attached to the RFP. Many agencies require an audited overhead statement from its own agency if available, or from another government agency. This is accepted as an interim overhead rate, subject to audit, and adjustment of the rate, based on the audit, at a later date. If the interim rate turns out to be higher than the actual audited rate, performed later, the Agency will have the right to recoup the "overpayment" at the interim rate and adjust it for the payment at the actual overhead rate, since overhead is a factor in the billing multiplier.

Profit: Profit rates are negotiated based on fair and reasonable profit for the market area the Agency operates in, for public sector work. A fair and reasonable profit may not be determined by simply applying a certain predetermined percentage to the total estimated direct cost. Profit factors, however, could be determined based on: Degree or risk, nature of the work to be performed, extent of the firm's investment, and subcontracting. This again, is a matter of policy and procurement requirements of the city and state where the Agency resides.

Simple Format Sample Fee Proposal – Architect /Engineer.

The format shown illustrates one phase of the design project. The process is repeated for the remaining phases.

Phase	Estimated Cost
Schematic Design	$ 46,000.00
Design Documents	$
Construction Documents	$
Bidding	$
Construction	$
Reimbursable Expenses:	$
TOTAL FEE	$

Sample Back-Up to Fee Proposal

Phase:	Schematic Design					
Position	Hrs	Direct Hourly Rate	Total Direct Labor	OH (150%)	Profit (15 %)	Total
Project Manager	40	$75	$3,000	$4,500	$1,125	$8,625
Architect	80	$60	$4,800	$7,200	$1,800	$13,800
Designer	120	$35	$4,200	$6,300	$1,575	$12,075
Drafter	160	$25	$4.000	$6,000	$1,500	$11,500
Total	400		$16,000	$24,000	$6,000	$46,000

Multipliers

Sometimes an agency may ask for a multiplier to be used with direct hourly rates to determine the fee. A multiplier is an application of the product of overhead and profit to direct labor. In the above example, the multiplier would be calculated as follows:

Direct Labor: 1.0
Overhead 1.5
Subtotal: 2.5

The subtotal is multiplied by the proposed fee as follows: 2.5 x 1.15 = 2.875 multiplier. In the above example, the Project Manager's direct rate would be multiplied by the multiplier to get the total cost for this position: $75.00 x 2.875 = $215.63 x 40 hours =$8,625

Design Cost Proposal Issues

The author has seen fee proposals for design services skewed because of ambiguity, particularly in two areas of service. The first is the time required for attendance at meetings. The Agency will want to have periodic project meetings, but may not be clear on the extent of time required for these meetings. There should be a way for the proposer to quantify the level of effort. This could be done by requesting proposers to assume a specified number of meetings with the Architect and its consultants. If there is a need for more meetings, these can be compensated with a contingency on a time and material (hourly) basis.

The second issue comes up in the construction phase. The RFP is not always precise about the number of field visits anticipated by the Architect / Engineer, either for construction observation, periodic inspection, or progress meetings. Again, the RFP should be as specific as possible, and a contingency might be considered for additional services not contemplated in the RFP.

Sometimes and agency will take the position that the additional need for meetings is due to the performance of the design team, and that may be correct, and in this case it is incumbent on the designer to make whatever efforts are necessary to make the project function properly. This should not be a pretext however for not compensating your design team for additional services.

Simple Sample Format for Agency Construction Management
In this format the general conditions (direct labor of the CM staff) is estimated and the direct hourly salary rate is applied to come up with direct total labor. Then, the Contractor is requested to propose a fee percentage based on construction. In the sample below, the estimated direct labor is $256,000 and the estimated fee is $250,000 for a total fee of $506,600.

Phase: Position	Proposed Hours	Direct Hourly Rate	Total Direct Labor
Project Manager	1,000	$95.00	$95,000
Project Engineer	1,000	$70.00	$70,000
General Super	800	$ 65.00	$52,000
MEP Inspector	400	$50.00	$20,000
Scheduler	100	$45.00	$4,500
Clerical	1,000	$15.00	$15,000
TOTAL	4,300		$256,500

FEE as a Percentage of Construction: Cost: $5,000,000
Proposed Fee: $5,000,000 x 4% = $250,000
TOTAL COST EXCLUDING REIMBURSBLES: $506,500

An alternative way of pricing is to request a multiplier on the direct labor. As in the example above, the total cost of direct labor is $256,000. In this example, the proposer submits a multiplier for overhead and profit at 1.97. If this is applied to the direct labor, the total fee is as follows:

Total Direct Labor: $256,500 x multiplier 1.97 = $506,500
Additional costs for out-of-pocket expenses are billed directly to the Agency. Whether there is a markup on the use of specialty consultants or other expenses is a matter of negotiation with the Agency and the Agency's policies and restrictions.

Selection of Architect / Engineer and Construction Management Consultants

The factors that are considered in determining which of the competing proposers are best qualified for the contract are contained in the RFP's evaluation criteria. The Agency, by establishing the effective evaluation criteria, must clearly prioritize the components of services that they have requested. This means that there will be a common standard for to determining the merit of each proposal.

Selection Criteria

The Agency's project is unique. There are special circumstances and situations for every project. The proposer who wants to be the Agency's Construction Manager should demonstrate a complete understanding of the Agency's needs in having this project constructed. The proposal that is submitted should clearly demonstrate an understanding of challenges and solutions for the construction of the project. The Agency will form a review panel that will review each proposal and evaluate them against specific criteria. The evaluation criteria and the relative weight of each should be included in the RFP document. These criteria often include:

- Technical ability to perform
- Personnel qualifications
- Past experience in related project services delivery
- Past performance and references
- Cost / price analysis

In reviewing the criteria established for the review of a professional consultant's proposal, you will note that the cost criterion is only one of a number of criteria. Cost should never be the only factor in selecting a consultant for the project. It is certainly a factor, and costs can be negotiated under Best and Final Offer conditions.

Each criterion is assessed a weight, and that weight corresponds with the level of importance associated with the criterion's reference to the objective of the project. For example, if the highest level of importance is cost, the weight of each criterion might look something like this:

Sample Rating Criteria Weight

Company Information 5%

Proposed Services 5%

Experience and Qualifications 10%

Compensation and Fees 70%

References 10%

Total - 100%

Part of the evaluation process is the determination that proposals are "responsive". Responsive means that the respondent submitted the proposal and all required forms to the specified location by the specified date and time.

Proposals can only be evaluated and scored based on what has been submitted by the proposer and the published evaluation criteria. A selection panel or committee convened for the purpose of evaluating and scoring proposals should be selected from staff that: understand the need for the project, understand the project goals, understand the needs of the facility managers and other users of the facility. They need to carefully review the RFP and read all of the proposals that are distributed for evaluation.

Any panel member or evaluator that may have a conflict or appearance of a conflict of interest needs to disclose this for a determination of their continued participation.

Depending on the process of the Agency, the evaluation panel may decide to seek best and final offers from one or more respondents, or may request only one best and final offer. Respondents should not be given the opportunity to submit its best and final offer without the request of the Agency.

Scoring the proposal is the process of assigning values to results in a consistent, systematic way. Scoring therefore assigns a value to the criteria identified as critical for project success and for selection of the service provider.

Evaluating the RFP

When a proposer sets out to respond to an RFP, there are certain considerations that must be taken into account for the proposer to be a viable candidate for an award of the contract. There are many mistakes that are made in drafting a proposal to public agencies: These mistakes or deficiencies impact on the score given by reviewers:

- The proposal is not tailored for the project and the client, and may be an off the shelf "cut and paste" job. There may even be typos referencing other proposals or the wrong project. This simply shows the Agency that you haven't taken the time to learn about the Agency or the project.
- The proposal has not summarized the client's critical needs nor demonstrated how the proposer will meet these needs. A proposer who submits a proposal that does not address the client's needs should simply not win the contract.
- The RFP is too lengthy, and critical information is missed because it is buried somewhere in the mass of pages submitted. As a result, the evaluation panel has trouble identifying key points, or it is too much of an effort to find them.
- The Executive Summary is not compelling, or has been omitted. The Executive Summary should focus the Agency reviewers on the key points, and then follow through in the technical approach.
- The proposer has not followed instructions for formatting and content, including page limits, submittal of required documents and forms.
- Past performance submitted is omitted or not relevant to the project under consideration.
- Evaluation criteria are not referenced in responses, making it difficult to relate the proposal to each criterion.

- The proposal does not evidence a clear understanding of the project, the challenges and the solutions.
- There are non compliance issues with the technical components of the proposal.

There are other factors that will go into your evaluation of a proposal, geared directly to specified criteria stated for evaluation:

(a). **Screening for eligibility.** Are there financial statements, questionnaires or other documents required to determine eligibility? Does the proposal address the proposer's eligibility for consideration?

(b). **Organization strength.** Is the organization viable for the services that will be provided? Does the organization have professional standing? Is there documentation that demonstrates that there is a sufficient track record of related experience and performance? Does the organization have a presence in the project area and can it provide services in the geographic area of the project.

(c). **Staff.** Do key personnel have the expertise and experience to perform on this project, and will they be available for the project when it starts?

(d). **Financial condition:** Do financial statements show fiscal strength? Are there adverse audit findings provided by other agencies? Are there liens or lawsuits pending?

(e). **Technical approach.** Is the technical approach provided realistic and innovative? Does it address particular requirements of the work proposed, and show a practical and feasible methodology? Is the timetable proposed for the project realistic? Is there a quality assurance program in place?

(g). **Utilization.** If the proposal has utilization goals for minority owned business enterprises (MBEs), woman owned businesses enterprises (WBEs), disadvantaged business enterprises (DBEs), etc., is there a utilization plan, and meaningful participation, as required?

Proposal Scoring Methodologies

There are methods that can be used by the selection panel to assign values to the various criteria.

The qualitative scoring methodology assigns a qualitative assessment the proposal relative to each criterion. The pre-determined designations such as poor, *fair, good,* and *excellent* may be used.

Example of Qualitative Scoring Methodology

Excellent = Exceeds expectations

Good = Above expectations

Fair = Meets Expectations

Poor = Does not meet expectations

N/R = Non-responsive

Quantitative scoring methodologies assign a numerical value to the respondent's ability in comparison with the criteria.

Example of Quantitative Scoring Methodology

4= Exceeds expectations

3= Above expectations

2= Meets Expectations

1= Does not meet expectations

0 = Non-responsive

Let's assume that the criteria established for a proposal were: past performance, technical approach, and past experience. Using this methodology, the following vendors were rated as follows:

Vendor	Past Performance	Technical Approach	Financial Capability
Proposer A	Fair	Excellent	Good
Proposer B	Poor	Good	Fair
Proposer C	Excellent	Non Responsive	Excellent
Proposer D	Excellent	Poor	Good

The scores assigned under this method are:

Vendor	Past Performance	Technical Approach	Financial Capability	Total Score
Proposer A	2	4	3	9
Proposer B	1	3	2	6
Proposer C	4	1	4	9
Proposer D	4	2	4	10

Under this process, the apparent designation would go to Vendor D, with 9 points. The rankings would be as follows:

Qualitative / Quantitative Not Weighted

1. Proposer D

2.. Proposer C / Proposer A

3. Proposer B

Sometimes the process will use a "Weighted Score". This allows the selection panel to assign more weight to a criterion that is provided more importance in the selection consideration than other criteria.

Interviews and Oral Presentations

To properly evaluate proposals, respondents may be requested to make an oral presentation to the committee. The respondent's original proposal cannot be changed during an oral presentation. All respondents must be afforded equal time in making their presentation. Proposers can, however, be asked to clarify the proposal or provide additional information.

Time slots for oral presentations are at the Agency's discretion. It can also be established by the drawing of lots. Interviews are to be conducted and controlled by the committee chairperson. All members of the evaluation committee should be present at the oral presentations. If oral presentations/interviews are anticipated at the onset of the RFP process, the RFP should specify anticipated dates, evaluation criteria and scoring methodology in the RFP.

The author has been at countless presentations when a panel member comes in late. This compromises the process and is unfair to all of the proposers. Being a member of the selection panel and attending during presentations should be the most important task of the day. There is no excuse for compromising the process by being late or skipping a presentation.

Although the proposals have already been scored, the panel has the right to make adjustments based on the oral presentation, provided that the evaluation continues to be based on the existing stated criteria of the RFP.

It is also advisable to require offerors to present the team that will actually be working on the project, so that you can better assess their experience, demeanor and qualifications. It makes no sense just to have corporate officers presenting, because they are not the persons with whom you will be interacting on a day to day basis. You are not merely looking for a sales pitch. You want to know who will be carrying out the functions of the project.

The next step is for the revaluation panel members to get together, discuss the proposals and presentation merits, and arrive at final scoring.

Negotiations/Best and Final Offer

Agencies have procedures in place for Best and Final Offers (BAFO). After the initial evaluation of proposals, the Agency may want to have discussions with proposers who have been determined to be reasonable candidates for award. The BAFO is generally requested when additional information is needed in order to make a decision, or all cost proposals are too high. This must be a structured process. All offerors who are requested to provide a BAFO needs to be given a fair opportunity to submit revised proposals, and a set of instructions for preparing this, indicating the areas of the RFP to be addressed and establishing a deadline for submission of the BAFO.

Vendor Award

The determination for contract award is a result of the scoring and BAFO process. After best and final offers are received, scores are adjusted and reported to the evaluation committee members. At a final meeting, the committee discusses the new information and selects the proposal that provides the best value for the Agency, city or state. A recommendation of award letter is issued to the newly selected proposer. This letter explains that their proposal is recommended for award. However, the final authorization has yet to be received by the executive management of the Agency. The letter should request for all insurance and bonds to be submitted to the Agency by a specified date. The letter should also state that failure to submit requested information by the deadline is just cause for contract forfeiture.

Notification

After executive approval is received along with all requested documentation from the vendor, a notice to proceed is sent to the vendor(s). This letter states that the vendor(s) was selected for award and thereby officially entered into contract with the Agency. The vendor(s) is now expected to provide the work defined in the RFP.

Chapter 3 References

The following sources were utilized in writing this chapter:

Andrew M. Civitello, Jr. Third Ed 2000. McGraw-Hill Companies, New York, NY

Schexnayder, C., and Mayo, R. Construction Management Fundamentals. McGraw-Hill 1st Edition. 2004

Various RFP documents issued by public agencies and authorities in New York State.

Chapter 4
Affirmative Action
Business Utilization and Employment

Affirmative Action – A Brief History

The effectiveness of **affirmative action programs** in the United States has been the subject of debate since the inception of the programs. Some have argued that programs that are designed to reverse the effects of past and present discrimination are themselves a form of discrimination because they give one group advantages of enjoying a preferred status over other groups based on race, ethnicity and gender.

While many see affirmative action as a way of taking steps to increase the representation of woman and minority group members, as well as other protected classes in the fields of employment, utilization of businesses owned or controlled by these groups, and education from which they have been excluded in the past, and as a means to attain equality and inclusiveness, critics of affirmative action see these programs as a quota-based system that is not fair and in fact demeans the very groups that they serve.

Public agencies administer affirmative action programs in order to enhance the participation of minority and female group members on publicly funded projects. In agency contracting, contractors and subcontractors are legally required to adopt affirmative action programs, so that public funds are not provided to vendors who discriminate against employees on the basis of race, color, creed, religion, sex or national origin. Agency affirmative action programs promote the utilization of firms that are owned and controlled by minority and female group members. Their participation is either promoted by being afforded subcontracting opportunities with firms that are majority owned, or by bidding work as prime contractors and prime consultants.

Affirmative action promotes equal opportunity. Affirmative action is a collection of policies that take into consideration the factors of race, color, religion, sex, and national origin, and other factors that have expanded the "protected classes" on the premise that these groups have been underrepresented. The attempt to improve their representation in employment, business, and education is at the expense of the majority group that has not experienced this exclusion historically. Affirmative action programs were based on the premise that the disadvantages associated with discrimination needed to be overcome, and that the workforce of public agencies and contractors were representative of the community.

Initially, affirmative action was a tool utilized to address inequality for African Americans. John F. Kennedy, in 1961, issued Presidential Executive Order 10925. This executive order mandated that there would not be discrimination in employment based on race, creed, color or national origin. In effect, at that time, the "protected class" was African American group members. Over time, affirmative action was expanded to include many other protected class members, including Hispanics, Asians, Pacific Islanders, Native Americans, the Asian subcontinent, women, the handicapped, disabled veterans, and other groups.

Affirmative Action programs met with resistance, with charges of "reverse discrimination". The Philadelphia Plan was implemented in 1969 under the Nixon Administration. The Plan resorted to strict quotas and timetables to address institutional discrimination as it applied to construction trade unions in Philadelphia.

There is a long legal history establishing Affirmative Action, beginning with the Equal Protection Clause of the 14th Amendment of the Constitution, in 1866, and the landmark Brown v. Board of Education Supreme Court Decision in 1954, ruling that separate educational facilities were "inherently unequal" and a violation of the 14th Amendment.

Landmark legislation followed in 1964 with the passage of **Title VII of the Civil Rights Act** of 1964, 42 USC 2000e, making it unlawful for an employer to hire or discharge any individual, or otherwise to discriminate against any individual with respect to his/her compensation, terms, conditions or privileges of employment, because of an individual's race, color, religion, sex or national origin. This covers hiring, firing, promotions and all workplace conduct.

Another important milestone, particularly as it relates to construction, was the signing of Presidential Executive Order 11246, in 1965, and later amended by Executive Order 11375. These executive orders prohibited federal contractors and subcontractors from discriminating against employees of applicants for employment on the basis of race, skin color, religion, gender, or national origin. The order further required contractors to take affirmative action to ensure that these protected classes are employed when they are available in the labor market. It also set standards based on size of companies triggering the requirement of written affirmative action plans, and goals and timetables for the utilization of women and minority group members were required. The goals were established by comparing the current workforce to the availability of women and minority group members in the Contractor's labor market area.

In 1969, President Richard Nixon issued Executive Order 11625, which established an Office of Minority Business Enterprise (MBE) in 1969. This office established programs to provide technical and management assistance to MBE firms and disadvantaged businesses, and established demonstration projects. Federal agencies were now mandated to actively administer affirmative action programs in federal contracting.

Later, President James Earl Carter signed Executive Order 12138 in 1979 establishing a National Women Business Enterprise (WBE) policy to support affirmative action for woman owned businesses.

Affirmative action programs were subject to various legal challenges. In the Regents of the University of California v. Bakke 438 U.S. 265 (1968), a medical school applicant filed a lawsuit, claiming reverse discrimination due to affirmative action admission policies.

Another milestone case was Adarand Constructors v. Pena, 515 U.S. 209 (1995). Adarand submitted the lowest bid to a general contractor for a government highway project. The general contactor awarded the job to Gonzales Construction, a disadvantaged business enterprise (DBE), due to affirmative action requirements of the state Department of Transportation that allowed for a financial incentive to the general contractor for hiring the DBE. Adarand filed suit against the Agency, and alleged that financial incentives for hiring such companies was unconstitutional. The court found that racial classifications must be analyzed under a strict scrutiny standard and such classifications are constitutional only if they are narrowly tailored measures that advance compelling governmental interests. The applicable standard of review is not determined based on which party is discriminated against, but on the basis of whether there is discrimination at all. All racial classifications under the Equal Protection Clause of the Fifth Amendment are analyzed under strict scrutiny; and a Fifth Amendment classification encompasses the same analysis as Fourteenth Amendment cases.

The Court held that "good intentions alone" are insufficient to sustain a supposedly benign racial classification. Essentially, the Department of Transportation could not simply enact this requirement on an assumption that those benefitting from special preferences are somehow less qualified and therefore need government intervention. The Court held that such practices hindered race based issues, and did not help them, and required that there must be detailed judicial scrutiny to ensure that there is no infringement on anyone's constitutional rights regardless of race. The Court required a "compelling" government interest, in order to enact this type of program. This ruling now required agencies to provide strict scrutiny standards for racial classifications under stringent conditions established by the Court.

Over time there have been many other court challenges to affirmative action, and a myriad of executive orders and regulations that have expanded the reach of affirmative action to a greater pool of protected classes. Judicial rulings have had a primary affect of removing from government contracting quotas for employment. These have been replaced by goals that are not quotas. Some jurisdictions, including the state of New Jersey, have moved toward race neutral programs such as Small Business Enterprise (SBE) programs based on company size and not ownership by a protected class member.

As described above, the federal government took the lead in affirmative action programs. States accept federal funding for their capital programs. As a result, state programs in many ways mirrored the federal requirements, either as a condition of receipt of federal funds, or for other reasons. As states enacted their own programs, state funds passed through cities, counties and municipalities. As recipients of state funds, these entities were required to meet state goals for affirmative action, as a condition of funding. Local governments have also enacted affirmative action programs of their own, where they use tax levy funds and other local revenues to fund construction.

MBE / WBE / DBE Utilization

As previously stated, affirmative action programs on public projects not only address equal employment opportunity for project labor, but also the utilization of firms that are minority owned business enterprises (MBE), woman owned business enterprises (WBE), and disadvantaged business enterprises (DBE). There can also be utilization programs that are race and gender neutral, such as programs and set asides for small business enterprises (SBE), veterans and disabled veterans, local business enterprises, and so on.

The goal of MBE/WBE/DBE programs is to assure that these firms are given the opportunity to participate in contract and procurement for supplies, construction, equipment and services. Under these programs, which must comply with the principles of the Adarand case cited above, goals are established for MBE /WBE and DBE firms.

"Good faith efforts" have replaced quotas for utilization of these firms. Agencies generally require contractors to demonstrate that good faith efforts were attempted to utilize MBE/WBE/DBE firms. Good Faith efforts are activities by a recipient or its prime contractor to increase MBE/WBE/DBE awareness of procurement opportunities through race/gender neutral efforts. The actions constituting "good faith effort" include:

- Efforts to ensure that MBE/WBE/DBEs are made aware of contracting opportunities to the fullest extent practicable through outreach and recruitment activities.
- Maintaining and updating a listing of qualified MBE/WBE/DBEs that can be solicited for construction, equipment, services and/or supplies.
- Outreach to appropriate sources within the company's geographic area and State to identify qualified firms for placement on agency MBE/WBE/DBEs business listings.

- Utilizing other MBE/WBE/DBE listings such as those maintained by state, city, county and local equal opportunity offices.
- Make information of forthcoming opportunities available to MBE/WBE/DBE firms and arrange time for contracts and establish delivery schedules. This includes, whenever possible, posting solicitations for bids or proposals for a minimum of 30 calendar days before the bid or proposal closing date.
- Advertise through the minority media in order to facilitate MBE/WBE /DBE utilization. Such advertisements may include, but are not limited to, contracting and subcontracting opportunities, hiring and employment, or any other matter related to the project.
- Advertise in general circulation publications, trade publications, State agency publications and minority and women business focused media concerning contracting opportunities on your projects. Maintain a list of minority and/or women owned business-focused publications that may be utilized to solicit MBE/WBE/DBEs.
- Perform an analysis to identify portions of work that can be divided and performed by qualified MBE/WBE/DBEs.
- Provide MBE/WBE/DBE trade organizations with succinct summaries of solicitations.
- Provide interested MBE/WBE/DBE firms with adequate information about plans, specifications, timing and other requirements of the proposed projects.

If a majority owned firm demonstrates that it has made "good faith efforts" to locate qualified MBE/WBE/DBE firms and none can be identified to provide specific technical work, then they are usually allowed to request a waiver on meeting goals. These waiver requests must be carefully reviewed, along with documentation and compared to the Agency's data base of certified firms.

Minority Business Enterprise and Woman Owned Business Enterprise.

Minority business enterprise and a woman owned business enterprise are for profit companies performing a commercially useful function. The business must have one or more minority or female owners with controlling interest. States and other government entities have equal employment offices that provide for certification of eligibility, in order to confirm that a minority or women-owned business is a credible meeting the following criteria:

- The owner is a citizen or lawful permanent resident of the United States and as applicable, the jurisdiction of the certifying agency.

- The owner is a member of an ethnic and disadvantaged group such as: Black American, Hispanic American, Asian-Pacific American, Native American, Asian-Indian American or Woman.

- The business is organized for profit, and a minority or woman owns and controls 51 percent of the business.

- A sole proprietor controls 100 percent of the business enterprise, and in corporations and partnerships minority owners control at least 51 percent of the management and daily business operations. Control is comprised of two parts; managerial and operational. The minority or women owner(s) must demonstrate responsibility for the critical areas of the operations and must be able to make independent and unilateral business decisions. The owners of these firms must demonstrate that each independently makes basic decisions in daily operations. Ownership and control by minorities and women must be real, continuing and shall go beyond the pro-forma ownership of the applicant as reflected in ownership documents.

- The business enterprise may be required to have operations physically located in the state.
- Some agencies have now imposed income standards including the net worth of a business owner, in determining MBE or WBE status. This is a relatively new criterion that has been added by some jurisdictions.

Often, an agency will provide goals for MBE/WBE participation. For example, a "goal" might be established for 5% WBE participation and 15% MBE participation. The smaller the contract, the less of an impact such goals have in benefitting such firms. Sometimes agencies apply the goals even if the resulting participation is so small that it is difficult to administer the project by delegating a percentage to an MBE or WBE firm. The author has seen solicitations for resident engineering services that might require only one resident engineer and one construction inspector, but with MBE and WBE goals. How does a prime consultant make a good faith effort in providing in this case, other than job sharing part of one position?

Other options that some agencies take and others do not are setting aside solicitations for small firm based on the size of the firm. In these cases, the set asides are "race neutral" but actually benefit MBE and WBE firms that fall into that size standard.

Another approach is to break up larger projects and allow small businesses, including MBE and WBE firms to compete. In construction trade contracting, bonding requirements might be waived or not required.

Disadvantaged Business Enterprises (DBE)

Disadvantaged Business Enterprise (DBE) goals are established for programs that contain federal funds. Recipients of U.S. Department of Transportation Federal Financial Assistance, who are primarily the 50 state highway, transit and airport agencies, are subject to Title 49 Code of Federal Regulations, parts 26 (49CFR26).

The U.S. Department of Transportation's DBE Program helps for-profit small businesses in which socially and economically disadvantaged individuals own at least a 51 percent interest and control management and daily business operations to compete for government contracts. It does this by requiring state and local transportation agencies to establish goals for DBE participation. Typically, the various transportation agencies in a state certify DBE firms, applying applicable federal regulations. To reduce the burden on DBE firms and agencies, many jurisdictions have a "unified certification" program, so that only one agency needs to perform the certification and it is recognized by other state agencies.

There are different requirements for DBE certification than for MBE and WBE certifications. There is a presumption that members of certain groups are disadvantaged, including citizens or legal permanent residents who are also women, black Americans, Hispanic Americans, Native Americans, Asian-Pacific Americans, Subcontinent Asian-Pacific Americans, or other minorities as determined by the Small Business Administration (SBA). Individuals who own and control their own businesses, but who do not fall into one of the above-listed predetermined categories, bear the burden of establishing their social and economic disadvantage before they may qualify for DBE status.

The presumption of disadvantage alone is not sufficient to qualify a business for DBE status. The applicant must also show that: (1) the firm is a small business, i.e., that its annual gross receipts do not exceed the cap set by the SBA to qualify as a small business; (2) the disadvantaged owner's personal net worth does not exceed a specified amount; (3) the business is not tied to another firm in such a way as to compromise its independence and control; and (4) the disadvantaged owner seeking certification possesses the power to direct or cause the direction of the management and policies of the firm.

In 2010, in order to qualify for certification, an owner had to have a personal net worth that did not exceed $750,000, excluding the owner's primary residence and the value of their ownership interest in the firm that is seeking DBE certification. There are also revenue limits for firms owned by the DBE applicant that may not be exceeded. There is no question that firms that are DBE certified have been provided with opportunities to participate on large and small scale highway, bridge, roadway, rail and other infrastructure projects that they would not have had if not for the program. Eventually, DBE firms that are successful may exceed the revenue standard for continued DBE certification and they are "graduated" from the program. Some of these firms go on to grow their companies to moderate or large sizes, and they are the DBE success stories. Other firms actually make business decisions whether or not to graduate, for a number of reasons:

- Although they have performed successfully as subconsultants on transportation projects, the agencies do not credit them fully for subconsultant work, and now these firms have to compete with prime contractors with greater experience and resources.
- These firms have not held prime contracts for large construction contracts and therefore continue to be at a disadvantage in the ability to compete.
- There is no bridge program to help DBE graduates to move into the realm of prime contractors, and many feel that graduation is like "falling of a cliff". As one owner once said, "As soon as we graduated the phone stopped ringing".

Section 8a Program

The federal Small Business Administration administers the 8(a) Business Development Program. This is a business assistance program for small disadvantaged businesses. Firms must be owned and controlled at least 51% by socially and economically disadvantaged individuals. The program also allows for teaming arrangements under its Mentor-Protégé Program that allows teaming between starting 8(a) companies and larger more experienced businesses. Participation is divided into two phases over nine years: a four-year developmental stage and a five-year transition stage.

Under this program, participants can receive sole-source contracts, up to a ceiling of $3 million for goods and services.

To qualify for the program, a small business must be owned and controlled by a socially and economically disadvantaged individual. Under the Small Business Act, this is defined to include certain presumed groups include African Americans, Hispanic Americans, Asian Pacific Americans, Native Americans, and Subcontinent Asian Americans. Other individuals can be admitted to the program if they show through a "preponderance of the evidence" that they are disadvantaged because of race, ethnicity, gender, physical handicap, or residence in an environment isolated from the mainstream of American society. In order to meet the economic disadvantage test, all individuals must have a net worth of less than $250,000, excluding the value of the business and personnel residence. Successful applicants must also meet applicable size standards for small business concerns; be in business for at least two years; display reasonable success potential; and display good character. Although the two-year requirement may be waived, firms must continue to comply with various requirements while in the program.

Administration of Opportunity Programs by Public Agencies

Public agencies, depending on size and resources may have an "**opportunity programs**" unit or department that administers programs to promote opportunities for MBE and WBE firms. They may also monitor employment of female and minority group members on publicly funded projects and compliance with equal employment and related provisions of contracts with contractors, suppliers and vendors.

Establishment of MBE and WBE goals
Construction Contracting functions may include establishment of MBE and WBE utilization and EEO goals on construction projects of a certain size standard applicable to contracting, professional services and other procurements. **Goals** are not quotas, but require a good faith effort to reach them.

Outreach
Outreach to MBE and WBE firms through advertising, networking, conferences, and other mean to inform the community about upcoming construction contracts.

Contracting
Administration of Job Order type contracting, construction procurement designed for contracts for maintenance, repair, and small construction with time sensitive requirements, without bonding requirements.

Small Business Set Aside
Set aside programs for small businesses, including MBE and WBE firms.

Advocacy
Assist MBE and WBE firms in the dealings with the Agency, its

personnel and its prime contractors or consultants, in order to promote their participation.

Compliance
Review prime contractor, consultants and vendors in complying with EEO and MBE and WBE utilization goals by determining revenues of MBE and WBE firm as subcontractors and subconsultants in comparison with goals stated in the contract. Collect performance data and provide management reports for compliance and utilization.

Selection Panel
Participate on selection panels for the procurement of professional services, evaluating the proposer's plan for MBE and WBE utilization.

MBE and WBE Waiver Requests
Apparent successful bidders or offerors may request a waiver for MBE and WBE utilization. In these cases, this department may review efforts made to attain goals, review portions of work that were targeted for MBE and WBE utilization, and assess reasons stated for the waiver request.

Issues in the Administration of Affirmative Action Programs

There is ample evidence that affirmative action programs implemented by public agencies have opened doors for MBE / WBE / and DBE firms. These contractors, professional consultants, service providers and supplies have been given the opportunity to compete for participation on public projects. Many of these firms have thrived and some have grown to the point where they no longer rely on these programs for the viability of their businesses. Other firms remain dependent on the program, and without goals established for their participation, they will struggle to remain in business.

In considering the history and the implementation of affirmative action programs in construction, key issues come to mind:

- Do affirmative action programs assist MBE/WBE/DBE firms in overcoming impediments to their success?

- Should MBE/WBE/DBE firms continue to rely on affirmative action utilization programs as part of their business model, or should the programs strive to provide these firms with sufficient experience, revenue and the opportunity for growth that their reliance on these programs can diminish over time?
- Do affirmative action programs help firms to participate in meaningful ways on construction programs? Are the goals sufficient to allow these firms to provide a commercially useful function that allows the firm to hire educated, trained and experienced staff and to assemble a portfolio of project experience and business references, and the financial means to compete on projects and to grow the company?
- Do public agencies do enough to create opportunities for MBE/WBE/DBE firms?

Fraud and Abuse

With more than 6.5 million privately owned firms, more than 89 percent of them are owned by white principals, including 62 percent of these are owned by white males, according to the U.S. Census Bureau. The affirmative action programs discussed in this chapter have been designed to reduce the imbalance that this poses in participation in public sector opportunities. Large non-minority and non – woman owned businesses that are awarded contracts are expected to make the "good faith effort" to provide a percentage of work, as specified in the awarded contract to MBE, WBE or DBE certified firms. The way things are supposed to work, bona-fide firms that meet MBE, WBE or DBE criteria register as such and are certified by public agencies to have these designations, making them eligible to partner of receive subcontracts and share in the work. Ever since the start of these programs, there has been the occasion of fraud and abuse. Recent examples have been found in the cities of Chicago, Philadelphia and New York.

Of course, fraud and abuse that revolves around MBE, WBE or DBE status deprives legitimate firms from participating in programs, because public dollars have gone to fraudulent companies. Government entities and law enforcement have taken action to investigate and to try and eliminate fraud and abuse in utilization programs. For example, Chicago Mayor Rahm Emanuel permanently banned an electrical contractor from doing business with the city after it claimed to be woman-owned in order to obtain contacts valued in the millions. In New York and New Jersey, a major construction management firm was accused of falsely reporting to the Dormitory Authority of the State of New York that an MBE was performing 100% of the general conditions on a major construction project. It was alleged that the firm was secretly performing the work with its own forces and directly managing the project, while passing through payments to the MBE firm by placing some of its own long term employees on the payroll of the MBE. In this case, the MBE would issue a paycheck to those individuals for the work performed by the majority construction management firm. A major New Jersey based heavy civil construction firm agreed to pay a $22 million settlement on a project with the New York City Department of Environmental Protection for a similar alleged scheme.

Often, this type of fraud and abuse comes at the behest of non-MBE, DBE or WBE firms, but in the cases cited above, these firms were compliant in the fraud. Perhaps for every single occurrence of fraud, there are hundreds of examples where fraud and abuse do not occur. In order to maintain the integrity of these programs, agencies have become more proactive. Some ways that this is accomplished is by:

- Tracking payments to MBE/WBE/DBE firms and auditing to determine the level of work performed by these firms
- Comparing payroll records of individuals billed by prime and subcontractors on a project to determine if "checker boarding" of personnel is taking place
- Conducting on-site reviews of operations of MBE, WBE and DBE firms seeking pre-qualification to determine if they are leasing or own their own premises, own their own construction equipment, and have the resources to perform the work
- Determining the true ownership and management of MBE, WBE and DBE firms, including determining if there is sufficient experience and training of owners to manage construction
- Determining if MBE, WBE and DBE firms are "re-contracting" work to non-certified firms

Impediments to Success of the Program

MBE/WBE and DBE construction contractors have experienced impediments to the growth of their businesses:

- Estimating and Bidding – lack of experience in estimating, lack of competitive pricing ability, weak cost tracking methods, and the need to improve credit relationships with material suppliers
- Marketing and Networking – inability to devote time and resources to market skills to potential customers
- Cash flow difficulties that impede the ability to purchase materials and to maintain daily operations
- Lack of knowledge of the market impeding ability to get work
- Too small to handle the scope of work being bid by the Agency
- Inability to bond the work

To what extent does the Agency address these impediments in your affirmative action program? All agencies establish goals for participation and contractual requirements for good faith efforts to meet the goals of the program. Do these efforts go far enough?

Some agencies have developed creative programs to assist MBE/WBE and DBE firms in overcoming these impediments. They have created programs to:

- Provide training programs in business management practices, marketing, estimating, and other skills and have offered these to the MBE/WBE/DBE community
- They have sponsored networking programs to allow these firms to meet with majority owned contractors, design professionals and Construction Managers
- They have taken steps to carve out projects that are small enough to allow bidding by MBE/WBE/DBE firms
- They have created bonding assistance programs or waived bonding requirements altogether

The Objectives of the Agency's Affirmative Action Program

Agencies should periodically review the goals and objectives of their affirmative action programs and determine if the Agency program is having a beneficial impact on the MBE/WBE/DBE community. On one level, an agency establishes goals for its projects and then measures the attainment of these goals by the amount of dollars that are contracted or subcontracted to these firms with agency funds. As these programs continue year after year, MBE/WBE/DBE firms participate and do business directly as prime contractors or consultants or indirectly as subconsultants, subcontractors, and vendors. If these firms do not grow beyond these programs, but become dependent on them for the majority of their revenue, is this a successful program? To put it succinctly, should the objective be to provide MBE/WBE/DBE with subcontracts indefinitely, or should the objectives of the program include the ultimate growth of these firms so that they can compete without these programs?

Example – the DBE Program

State transportation agencies receive federal funds for their infrastructure projects, and administer DBE utilization requirements that are attached to federal funding. These programs are directed to contractors and professional consultants that provide design and resident engineering on highway, rail and bridge construction. In order to take advantage of this program, many engineering firms have been formed by female and minority group members who are considered to be socially disadvantaged, and if their personal wealth and revenues meet size standards, their companies can be certified as disadvantaged business enterprises. Any projects funded with federal money require the use of DBE firms, and goals are established. When times are flush and transportation agencies are busy, many DBE firms do quite well. In fact, some of them graduate the program eventually because their revenue increases to the point where they exceed the DBE size standard. Some firms want to graduate so that they are no longer dependent on the program. Others do not want to graduate, and make the DBE program their business model. They will try to manage their revenues so that they never graduate.

There are reasons why firms do not want to graduate. First, they fear that the phone will stop ringing from the large firms they are doing business with when their DBE status is gone, simply because those prime contractors and consultants will no longer receive DBE credit by going back to these firms, and will seek new DBE partners. This is often the case, even if the former DBE firm was a good partner and performer. The majority firm may want to work with these firms, but still need to carve out the DBE piece to a certified firm.

Another problem is that the state agency has a process for selection of prime consultants that takes into account the experience of a firm as a prime consultant, but devalues the experience of a firm that was a subconsultant. In this case, the graduating DBE consultant may have an extensive inventory of subcontracts with a particularly state agency, but now the firm needs to compete with majority owned firms that have much more extensive experience. Unless the Agency has a program that continues to aid the DBE graduate so that the firm can continue to work for the Agency, such as setting aside work for graduates, or lowering the requirements for selection for a project, what is the incentive to graduate?

Carving Out Opportunities to Compete as a Prime Contractor or Consultant

An MBE/WBE/DBE firm that has had an opportunity to perform work as a prime contractor or prime consultant with the Agency has a much better chance of winning more prime work with the Agency and other construction agencies than if it is only able to perform as a subcontractor or subconsultant. A firm that performs prime work will either develop or improve its capacity in management and staffing resources or will fail and not be able to obtain more work at the prime level. However, if the firm is successful and can develop a track record as a prime consultant, their reliance on affirmative actions programs can very well decrease.

An agency can advertise a $20 million construction project and seek a prime consultant, and establish goals for MBE or WBE participation, or perhaps could creatively break this project up into pieces, so that MBE and WBE firms can compete as prime consultants in a race and gender neutral small business set-aside bid.. This might create the opportunity for several firms who would never have a shot at prime work because of size requirements to successfully compete, and then pursue larger pieces down the road. Of course, this is more work for the Agency, is more costly, and requires more effort. At the same time, it is more creative and could have a substantial impact on the success of emerging firms.

Inability to Bond

Many public agencies have developed contracting **bonding assistance** programs to help small local contractors obtain bid, payment and performance bonds or increase their bonding capacity, to help them overcome the impediment to bid posed by bonding requirements. This type of assistance may be sponsored by the Agency or governmental entity and administered by a financial management firm. These types of programs may include consultations, workshops and seminars, and technical assistance to help contractors improve relationships with surety providers. Assessments of the company's financial strength and needs in order to obtain bonding may be provided.

Another initiative could take the form of an agreement by which a larger business agrees to indemnify the bond provided to the small business. A bond indemnification agreement would allow a small business to obtain a bond that it might not otherwise be able to obtain. Bonding indemnification arrangements between large and small businesses allow MBE/WBE/DBE firms to obtain construction work, without actually becoming affiliated firms.

Some agencies have taken steps to waive bonding requirements in order to allow smaller firms to bid work. Critics of this approach argue that sooner or later these firms will have to enter the bonding world, and waivers only delay realty. They also argue that public funds are at stake and the likelihood of unqualified contractors doing public work is enhanced through these types of programs. These arguments are countered by limiting the size of the project and exposure and by vetting and monitoring firms where the bonding requirement is being waived.

Some programs have been developed in the private sector to deal with bonding requirements. Owners and developers are seeking ways to avoid rising bond premiums, which translate eventually to higher project costs. Some Construction Managers and general contractors have given Owners an option through programs like "Subguard". This is an insurance product that replaces subcontractor bonds. Under this type of program, insurance policies are purchased by Construction Managers that obligate the insurance company to pay for costs incurred because of subcontractor default. These types of policies are offered for Construction Managers who are working "at-risk". If the Owner approves this arrangement, the subcontractors are added to the policy in lieu of posting bonds. This does not relieve the subcontractors from qualifying on the basis of past performance and financial strength in order to be covered under the program.

The main advantage for Owners and Construction Managers is lower cost of premiums coupled with more flexibility in resolving subcontractor defaults. The policies provide two main advantages over traditional bonds for both Owners and Construction Managers: lower premium costs and greater flexibility in addressing and resolving subcontractor defaults - which in turn avoids potential delays and related problems. Current bond premiums average 2 percent of contract costs, while Subguard premiums are closer to 1.25 percent. The disadvantage is that the Subguard insurer does not have a primary contractual obligation to step in and complete the job, as would be the case if there were a bonding surety in play. The risks are transferred to the Construction Manager based on a promise of payment for default by the insurance company. If a program like Subguard is presented to the Agency, the Agency needs to consider whether the Construction Manager offering such a program can manage the obligations inherent with the program and have the financial resources to make the program successful.

When Times Are Tough....A Case Study.

MBE contractors in a major south eastern city have endured a tough economic climate at the end of the first decade of the 21st Century. Times are tough for all firms in this climate, but tougher for them. Many are losing their businesses or on the brink, despite skill, experience and capability. Many of the city's minority contractors complain that there is systematic exclusion from large government contracts and that the MBE/DBE program has also failed them. One business owner commented that the programs do not work, stating "It's just a game the city plays." Another stated that qualified contractors are idle while work is available. This is despite the fact that there is an active school construction and transit program in the city with MBE and DBE goals. One licensed, bonded and insured minority contractor said, "All of them are doing work, but ain't none of us working". The complaint is that the same contractors keep getting the work.

Under the DBE program, a percentage of the work in this city that is federally funded provides for participation by DBE firms. One critic stated that the program looks good "on paper" but not in practice. These owners believe that there are no consequences for a lack of good faith and participation of these firms. Others complain that they are not finding out about bidding opportunities.

Some MBE contractors complain that when they are lucky enough to be hired as subcontractors, they often cannot get paid promptly because of contract disputes between the prime and the public agency that they are working for. They are often told to go to court and litigate. They complain that agencies do not follow the rules in place to protect them. They say that city agencies ignore regulations requiring subcontractors and vendors to be paid before final disbursement of funds to the prime contractor. Others complain about failure to receive prompt payment within a reasonable time after the prime receives a payment for work provided by the sub.

Many in this city believe that the situation will continue until public officials are held accountable. They believe that majority owned firms will continue to look out for their own interest, and that the minority community needs to step up and solve their own problems.

Chapter 4 References

The following sources were utilized in writing this chapter:

8(a) Business Development Program. Small Business Administration. Retrieved from http://www.sba.gov/aboutsba/sbaprograms/8abd/index.html

Duckett, M. Fade to Black. The Charlotte Post. October 14, 2010 Retrieved from http://www.thecharlottepost.com

Executive Order 11246. Retrieved from: www.archives.gov/federal-register/codification/executive-order/11246.html

Subguard. Retrieved from: www.zurichna.com/NR/rdonlyres/D8ABD9F0-95AE-4B06-B58C-1087399A2D46/0/Subguard.pdf

Title VII of the Civil Rights Act of 1964. Retrieved from: http://www.eeoc.gov/laws/statutes/titlevii.cfm

Chapter 5
Construction Contract Law

Contracts

Contracts and contract law are a dominant factor in the legal aspects of construction. A **contract** provides for a promise or promises, in exchange for payment. If the contract is breached, the law provides for a legal remedy. Contracts may be entered into, and involve risky agreements in regard to a project, as long as there is no violation of law or public policy.

In order for a contract to exist, the following conditions must be enforceable:

- There is a valid agreement between the parties
- The subject of the contract is lawful
- There is consideration for each promise (e.g. payment for performance of tasks)
- There is a legal capacity of each party to execute the contract
- All legal requirements as per the form of contract are complied with.

A **Breach of Contract** occurs when one party to the contract fails to provide what has been agreed to, without a valid excuse or justification. In this case, the injured party has a right to recover damages by seeking restitution for the breach.

Contractual Obligations

There are two different types of obligations in a contract. One type is **expressed obligation**, and the other is **implied obligation**. Expressed obligations are spelled out in black in white in the contract. Implied obligations are not written but understood to exist none the same. In construction, the following are examples of implied obligations:

- Each of the contracting parties will cooperate with the other's efforts to perform under the contract.
- The Owner will provide access to the site so that the Contractor can perform the work.
- A prime contractor will not delay or obstruct the work of its subcontractor or other prime contractors at the project site.
- The Owner warrants that the plans and specifications are constructable.

Order of Precedence

Order of Precedence provides that when there are two or more conflicting provisions that are not compatible, the rules of contract interpretation provides an order of precedence. Most likely this order of precedence is in the general conditions of the Agency's contract form. There are often conflicts in the construction documents between the specifications and the drawings. To address this type of issue, the order of precedence in the contract may state that the specifications will take precedence over the drawings, if there is a conflict or inconsistency. If there is no order of precedence provision, it has been a generally accepted common law rule of precedence that specific terms and provisions will take precedence over general terms and provisions.

Contract Ambiguity

Contract Ambiguity exists when the contract cannot meet the *plain meaning rule* that has been applied by the courts, meaning that the contract is not clear and unequivocal on its face. The risk of ambiguity accrues to the drafter of the contract unless the non drafting party knew of or should have known of the ambiguity. In order for the ambiguity to exist, there must be more than one reasonable interpretation of the contract as written. The non drafting party to the contract also must demonstrate that the ambiguous clauses were relied upon. If the ambiguity is latent, it means that the contract language has an underlying ambiguity that is not readily apparent from the language of the contract.

Duty to Inquire

If there is a patent ambiguity, this means that the ambiguity was so obvious that the non drafting party of the contract should have requested clarification. Some government agencies provide provisions requiring the Contractor to exercise the **duty to inquire** if there is a patent ambiguity, but the lack of this language does not relieve the Agency from responsibility for contract ambiguity.

Contract Negligence

Negligence is a lack of care and due diligence. It is part of the law of **torts.** A tort is a negligent or intentional civil wrong that is not the result of contract or law. It causes an injury for which the injured party may sue for damages. Negligence is invoked in cases where the Architect or Engineer does not meet professional standards and whose actions cause injury to others. It is also applicable for contractors who do not meet standards of the industry and cause injury or provide substandard work. The responsibility for competence goes beyond the requirements of any contract.

Each party to the construction project has distinct obligations to perform under their respective contract, whether the obligations of the contract are expressed or implied. For example, the General Contactor or Construction Manager should never assume the responsibilities of the Architect / Engineer. A well meaning contractor who wants to expedite the work cannot assume the responsibility for fixing the design, where the contract documents are not adequate for the work being performed. The Contractor's obligation is to coordinate and construct the work, not to coordinate the design. In a similar vein, the interpretation of the construction drawings and specifications rests with the Architect / Engineer and not with the Contractor or Construction Manager.

The Owner / Agency's Rights and Obligations

The contract that the Agency uses with the General Contractor cannot disclaim responsibilities that ordinarily would accrue to the Owner. Construction law has established, over time, that there are certain warranties, duties and responsibilities of the Owner, regardless of what is written into the contract by the Owner. Thus, the Owner, and by extension, the Agency is responsible for:

- Maintaining the integrity of the public bidding process, from evaluating the qualifications of proposers to the award of the contract to the apparent low bidder
- Funding the base contract and all changes
- Providing all surveys and data about the project site, and disclosing superior knowledge
- Warranting that the plans and specifications are adequate for construction of the project
- Ensuring that all required easements and site authorizations have been secured
- Acting within reasonable time periods so that the progress of work can meet the schedule
- Providing the final interpretation of the contract documents
- Assuming the responsibility of the Architect / Engineer

Upholding the Integrity of the Public Bidding Process

When the Agency is bidding work, it is charged with protecting the public trust by awarding contracts to the lowest responsible bidder. When disqualifying the lowest bidder, the Agency must be on solid ground, following the process in place for making that determination. The reasons for the disqualification must be able to stand up to a court challenge. When the bid is received by the Agency, it is accompanied by bid bonds, affidavits and statements concerning the integrity of the bidder, and other details as provided by the bid form that the Agency has issued. In making the award, the Agency must ensure that the bid submitted has met strict compliance with the terms of the bid documents. For example, if a late bid is accepted, the integrity of the competitive bidding system is compromised because the Agency has allowed the late bidder to have more time in preparing the bid, causing an unfair advantage to the other bidders.

Funding the Work

The Agency will have secured funding before issuing a request for proposal. Once the project is underway, the Owner must ensure that funds are available for timely payment, providing that the contractor has met all requirements. This is the case when quantities of materials have been delivered to the site and installed in accordance with the requirements of the contract. The Agency must also ensure that funds are available for changes to the work. Some public agencies build a 10% contingency pay item into the contracts for such events.

Providing Surveys and Data and Disclosure of Superior Knowledge

The Contractor relies on receipt of correct and accurate information. In order to properly layout and implement construction, property lines and contract limits need to be accurately delineated by the Owner. Following this basic premise, where there is to be subsurface work, boring data (subsurface material data) or other test data that describe subsurface material composition that will be encountered as part of the project must be disclosed. The Agency should not attempt to shift the risk for unknown subsurface conditions to the Contractor through complicated contract language. If there are extraordinary requirements in regard to subsurface conditions that require risk, the Contractor should be knowledgeable of the risk and determine the pricing accordingly, assuming a willingness to submit a bid under those circumstances.

Another issue is the accurate location of utilities on the site. Normally, the Owner will be responsible for this, requesting that the surveyor employed by the Owner provide a utility survey, which includes research of existing utility records and field verification of locations. If the utility information is not accurate and this requires such efforts as greater shoring, greater trench width or other activities that would substantially increase the Contractor's cost, it is likely that the Owner will be responsible for these costs.

Warranting the Plans and Specifications

Years ago, the Spearin Construction Company took the federal government to court when the company contended that the plans and specifications were defective, and therefore the Contractor should not be liable for additional costs that it was incurring due to these defects. In the United States v. Spearin, 248 U.S. 132 (1918), the Court determined that it was the responsibility of the Owner to warrant that the plans and specifications were adequate for construction. This does not, as we have discussed before, relieve the Contractor from a duty to inquire, where the error is obvious. Known as the "Spearin Doctrine", case law establishes that the

Architect or Engineer is the ultimate party responsible for design errors, but all parties have responsibility for identifying and minimizing the effect of such errors through prompt notification.

Easements and Authorizations

The Contractor must be provided access to the physical site as required to perform the work. Unless the contract specifically restricts access, the Contractor must be able to assume full access. This also means that the site is accessible for the transport of vehicles, material and equipment. Many times, public agency projects cannot accommodate all of the logistical needs of the Contractor at the site, such as adequate parking, storage of materials on site, restrictions of access to the site, etc. This needs to be clearly communicated in the bidding documents, so that the Contractor can price the accommodations that need to be made, such as off site storage, accordingly.

Acting Promptly on Changes and Clarifications

Speed is always of the essence. This is true for large public agencies when it comes to providing clarifications when they are required and reviewing and approving change orders. Change orders, if not addressed, disrupt the sequence of work, and thus they should be resolved as quickly as possible.

Providing Final Interpretation of Documents

The actual authority to provide final interpretation of the documents should be clearly specified in the contract documents. Ultimately, the contract is between the Contractor and the Agency, and therefore the Agency is the arbiter of the interpretation of the documents. Documents issued by the AIA may actually empower the Architect in this regard, but in public contracting, this is not the usual practice. The contract will also provide a disputes and resolution clause for final dispute resolution, with appeals to a higher authority.

Assuming Responsibility for Design Professionals

Professional liability is assumed by the Architect/Engineer for services they perform on the project. The Architect / Engineer are the agent of the Owner, and therefore the Owner has ultimate responsibility for the Architect. The Owner protects itself by requiring the Architect/Engineer to provide professional liability insurance.

The Architect / Engineer

As the agent of the Owner, the Architect / Engineer have responsibility for the technical design. The Agency, when it contracts with the designer, has put its faith and trust for the project in the hands of these professionals. Once the Agency transfers the design requirement to the Architect / Engineer, it should seek to avoid participation in the design work, with the exception of review of the work product. Otherwise the liability for design may be shared by the Agency and the Architect.

The American Institute of Architects (AIA) issues a library of construction documents that it has prepared with consultations of Owners, contractors, attorneys, architects, engineers, and others. These can be found on the AIA website, www.aia.org. Some believe these to be the industry standard, and is generally used by architects in privately funded work.

The general responsibilities of the Architect / Engineer are:

- The production and coordination of all drawings and specifications
- The technical accuracy of the design and construction documents
- Development of the design
- Compliance with laws, regulations and codes that apply
- Interpretation of the documents
- Submittal review and approval
- Response that is prompt and timely
- Evaluation of the Contractor's work
- Exercise of professionalism and judgment

Privity of Contract

The actual authority of the Architect / Engineer is contained in the contract. The term **"privity of contract"** is applicable in the contractual relationship between the Architect /Engineer and the Agency. A contract cannot impose obligation or assign rights under the contract to any other person or agent, other than the parties that have executed the contract. Only the parties to the contract can sue to enforce their rights or to claim damages. This means that the parties cannot enforce any obligations under the contract because they are not party to it. A contractor cannot sue a designer for deficiencies in the documents that cause injury to the Contractor. The Contractor has a contract with the Agency, and therefore must sue the Agency for breach of contract. In this case, the courts will apply expected professional standards to determine if there is liability.

The authority of the Architect / Engineer can be enhanced by the Owner based on the contract scope of services. For example, if the Architect / Engineer have the authority to perform construction phase inspections and supervisory functions, it becomes a special agent of the Agency, and takes on more responsibility than is described under the general responsibilities described above.

Production and Coordination of the Plans and Specifications

The Architect / Engineer is responsible to ensure that all items of work are provided in sufficient detail on the plans and specifications, in effect describing the complete project so that it can be built as intended by the design. The designer's responsibility cannot be shifted to the Contractor. Language indicating that the plan is "complementary" or that the Contractor must provide work whether or not it is fully described in the documents is an attempt to shift design responsibility, and such language should never be accepted by the Agency in its documents. As stated before, this does not relieve the Contractor from responsibility for inquiring about obvious mistakes or inconsistencies, but the Contractor is not obligated to pursue that inquiry further other than to notify the Agency.

Technical Accuracy of the Documents

The documents must be technically accurate, down to the horsepower specified for an electric motor. Likewise, a particular model boiler should fit where it is supposed to go. The Contractor should not be required to make it fit. The design must be workable and practical in order for the work to be installed or constructed as intended by the design.

Development of the Design

The design is in the purview of the designer, but there are times when a contractor will want the design modified because of sequencing or other benefits by altering means or methods. This may be because it benefits the Contractor, the project, or both.

When this happens, the Contractor is assuming responsibility for some aspect of the design if there is a change in design workability. The Contractor should be made aware of the risk it is assuming in this case.

Compliance with Applicable Laws, Regulations and Codes

The design must comply with all fire, safety and other applicable building codes. The Agency is entitled to a design that is fully compliant, and it is the responsibility of the Agency's design team to ensure that the facility will meet all applicable requirements.

Interpretation of Contract Documents

The Architect / Engineer are generally responsible for interpreting the documents for clarification and dispute resolution. This is often required when the contract documents are inadequately detailed or specified. It is not unusual for a contract to have a lack of specificity from time to time, requiring an interpretation of the contract requirements. Usually, the reasonable exercise of judgment results in the informal resolution of these types of issues. If the problem is intractable, the next steps are arbitration and litigation.

Review and Approval of Shop Drawings and Submittals

The review of data submitted by the Contractor, including shop drawings, product data and schedules by the Architect / Engineer is performed so that the Owner / Agency and the Architect / Engineer can obtain an understanding of how the Contractor plans to perform an aspect of the work. The Contractor therefore informs through the submittal of the processes, materials and methods to be used, and reflects the Contractor's understanding of the construction requirements.

In cases where the Architect /Engineer have approved shop drawings that deviate from the contract documents, courts have imposed liability on design professionals. This was the case when the Hyatt Regency multistory interior bridge collapsed in Kansas City in 1981, killing over 100 persons and injuring 186. The collapse was due to a faulty structural steel detail submitted in shop drawings and approved, and sealed by a professional Engineer.

Prompt and Timely Response

The Architect / Engineer must review and act upon these submittals within a reasonable time. Excessive delay can cause liability to the

Agency.

Evaluation of the Work

The Architect / Engineer have a responsibility to evaluate the work, and the actual level of evaluation or inspection will be specified in the scope of work of the consulting contract with the Architect / Engineer. While the Architect cannot be held responsible for every nut and bolt installed by a contractor, it would not be reasonable for the Architect to delay inspection until after most of the significant work is installed.

The Architect / Engineer, depending on the contract scope, may have responsibility for testing and inspection, including verification of the amount of work put in place by the Contractor, with corresponding payment value, rejecting non-conforming work, and other such responsibilities. This may be performed by the Construction Manager, if there is one on the site. The Contractor is still contractually obligated to install work as required by the contract and is not relieved of this responsibility.

Exercise of Professionalism and Judgment

It is expected that the Architect / Engineer has exercised due diligence, skill and judgment in performing professional services under your project. This is an *implicit warranty* of the contract that the Architect/Engineer holds with the Agency. The Contractor has the right to assume, absent a patent error, that the documents are complete and sufficient to install the work as designed and specified.

General Responsibility of the General Contractor

The general contractor is obligated under the contract to:

- Require bidders to inquire about the bid documents (duty to inquire)
- Plan, schedule and lay out the work
- Supervise and install the work
- Provide workmanship in accordance with industry standards
- Coordinate all aspects of the work
- Submit shop drawings
- Process contract payments to subcontractors and suppliers
- Provide required insurance
- Submit and implement the safety program

- Warranties

Duty to Inquire

As stated previously, the Contractor has a duty to inquire when the bidding documents are ambiguous or patently deficiencies. The Contractor is not obligated, however, to complete an exhaustive review of the site and available site data not provided. The Contractor is expected to provide for a reasonable review, but this does not mean a complete search of all available documents in order to uncover flaws or ambiguities in the documents. The Agency has implicitly warranted the adequacy of the plans and specifications.

Plan and Schedule the Work

The Contractor, with a workable design in hand, is expected to plan, schedule and sequence the work in a manner that meets the approved construction project schedule. The work will be physically laid out from survey data that has provided benchmark and baseline references, and assuming the data is correct, the Contractor is obligated to expedite this.

Supervise and Install the Work

The Contractor is contractually obligated to provide competent supervisory and qualified personnel to install the work. Progress must be consistent with the approved schedule. All methods and techniques to install the work are the obligation of the Contractor.

Submit Shop Drawings

Without timely submittal of shop drawings, the schedule cannot be met, because the Agency and its Construction Manager should not allow work to progress that requires approval of submittals. Shop drawings must be clear and comprehensive in describing details and products that are submitted for approval. Where there are differences between what the contract requires and what is submitted, the Contractor must highlight these so that they come to the attention of the Architect / Engineer.

Process Contract Payments to Subcontractors and Suppliers

The Agency contract requires the Contractor to pay its subcontractors and sub vendors so that they are paid when the general contractor is paid, within a reasonable time frame.

Provide Required Insurance

The Contractor is required to submit insurance required in the amounts specified in the contract, and to name the Agency and all additional parties that must be included. Coverage will include worker's compensation, general liability, and automobile insurance.

Contractor Safety Plan

The Contractor is required to submit a safety plan for review and approval. The program will require with OSHA standards, and will address such items as personnel protective equipment, warning signs, barricades, scaffolding, fire control, ladders and walkways, egress, and other requirements.

Warranties

The equipment and materials installed and workmanship by the Contractor will be warranted for a specified period of time. The Contractor will also provide guarantees and warranties from manufacturers for materials and equipment provided.

Key Contract Principles

Scope of Work

The scope of work should clearly establish the work that will be performed on the contract. This does not mean that there has to be an exhaustive description of the scope, but there should be references to the contract documents themselves. The scope does not only address the technical work, but also the responsibilities the Contractor has for the facilities and for the administration of the contract.

Reasonable Review

Throughout this textbook, we have used the word "reasonable". A *reasonable review* by the Contractor means that all bid and contract documents have been reviewed as they relate to the Contractor's work. What can be visibly seen or reasonably inferred gets priced in the bid. If the Contractor is aware of patent errors, these must be disclosed to the Agency. It is not the Contractor's obligation to discover mistakes, inconsistencies or other problems through a complete search of documents to identify problems with the documents. That should occur in the pre-construction phase with design and constructability reviews.

Pass Through Principle

Prime consultants providing professional services use subconsultants, as required and prime contractors use subcontractors. Contract privity exists between the Agency and the prime contract holder. However, under the **pass through principal**, subconsultants are responsible to the Architect or Construction Manager, and subcontractors are responsible to the general contractor in the same way that these prime consultants and contractors are responsible to the Agency as contract holder. Many consultants and contractors in fact attach the prime contract to the subcontract documents.

Change Clause

Changes are a fact of life. Conditions are discovered that were unknown, the scope changes due to a program change, the documents didn't address an item of work sufficiently. These and other circumstances result in changes. The construction contract contains a change clause because changes are expected, and there needs to be a mechanism to continue work while changes are addressed.

Under the change clause, the Agency can order additional work or delete work and take a credit. Changes can be made in sequencing, timing, quantity, or methods. The changes are processed with a **change order**. The contract will usually address means of compensation with pricing for the changes. For example, in a masonry contract, prices per unit may decrease as quantities increase, and vice versa. However, where the contract does not address predetermined pricing, it is important that records are maintained to document cost so that agreement on compensation can be reached. Time issues are negotiated concurrently with cost negotiations, if additional time is sought.

Claims and Disputes

Contract clauses for claims and disputes have a process for timely notification to the Agency in order for the claim to be recognized as such. Claims can be resolved informally or formally. Claims must be carefully prepared, developing an administrative file that present documentation of events leading to the claim, and documentation of costs associated with the claim. Delay is often a component of claims. When this occurs, CPM scheduling analysis is often employed to determine the merits of claims involving the schedule. Demonstrative evidence is also employed to support claims, including photographs, charts, graphs and other visual documentation. The qualities of documents submitted with a claim have a bearing on whether the claim is determined to be valid. There are federal and state rules of evidence that work in favor of the claimant or defender against the claim, especially when the documents are bona fide business records, meaning that they have been regularly maintained, prepared by knowledgeable persons, and have been contemporaneously kept. Claims that are adequately documented and presented to tell the story of the claim are more likely to be resolved earlier, and informally.

The contract may provide for alternative dispute resolution, which stops short of litigation. There are other resolution methods short of litigation, including the use of dispute resolution boards. Arbitration is another method, and it is binding. Mediation is not binding. The ultimate, most costly and time consuming way to resolve the dispute is litigation.

Contract Termination

All contracts recognize the right to terminate a contract based on default. The Agency, as the non breaching party to the contract, has the right to seek damages resulting from termination from the Contractor's surety. This is usually the result of a material breach of the contract. Generally, minor deviations from the contract, which in themselves may result in damages, do not rise to the level of a breach of contract and termination.

Federal standards, which are often mirrored in other contract documents, provide for termination when a contractor has failed to perform by a specified date, produce defective or non compliant work, or refuse to prosecute the work in a diligent effort to meet the schedule.

In the case of default terminations, the contract provides a procedure to contest the termination. There are also "termination for convenience" clauses that are found in public agency contracts. In this case, payments are usually limited to compensation for work in place and do not include lost or unrealized profit.

When there is a termination by default, the Agency may elect to:

- Complete the work itself
- Hire a new contractor to complete the work
- Allow the defaulted contractor's surety to complete the work. In this case, the surety is obligated up to the amount covered by the bond

Chapter 5 References

The following sources were utilized in writing this chapter:

Civitello, A. Construction Operations Manual of Policies and Procedures. Third Edition. 2000. McGraw-Hill Companies. New York, NY.

Encyclopedia of American Law. Edition 2. 2008. The Gale Group

Kelleher, T., Editor. Smith, Currie and Hancock's Common Sense Construction Law. 2005. John Wiley & Sons. Hoboken, NJ

Smith, Curry and Hancock's Common Sense Construction Law. John Wiley & Sons, 2005

Al Palumbo

CHAPTER 6
PROJECT LABOR
Unions and Prevailing Wage
Project Labor Agreements

Union and Non Union Construction

In the 21st Century, labor unions in the construction industry have seen the share of jobs going to companies that employ union workers in the trades drop significantly. In New York City, for decades a union town, it is estimated that two out of five construction jobs in 2013 are non-union. In the private market, employers are looking for concessions from unions, seeking reductions in labor costs, through reductions in benefits and work rules.

In metropolitan areas that experienced a construction boom, there was enough work to go around in the construction industry. The fact that non-union companies were increasingly obtaining a share of the work did not have much of an impact on employment of union trades persons. This did not stop unions from picketing these work sites, and in New York City, placing a large inflatable rat in front of the project site. As construction commodities and land prices escalated, some developers looked to save money on labor costs. The unions and employers, who are parties to collective bargaining agreements where all employees of the company who work in the trades are union members, make the case that union laborers are more skilled and safer than their non-union counterparts. In the years after 2000, non-union companies began to see more market share for midsized construction, and this is where most of the unions have been losing their share of the market. In New York City, the union wage for a carpenter in 2011 was $46 per hour. When other benefits are added, the total cost per hour was $85 dollars. Other union trades, including Laborer, could earn a salary rate of over $50 per hour. On some non-union jobs, carpenter and laborer salaries varied, but were often not even close to the union wage scale, sometimes earning as little as $10 - $30 per hour with or without benefits. On public sector jobs, non union labor is required by law to receive the pay and cash equivalent of benefits equal to the prevailing wage.

Collective Bargaining Agreements

Employers who hire union trades personnel sign **collective bargaining agreements** with the unions that represent these trades. A collective bargaining agreement is a contract that is set for a term of one or more years between employers and the employees who are represented by an independent trade union. It is a contract that is enforced by law that establishes wages, hours of work, working conditions, overtime, holiday and vacation pay, and other benefits.

Force Account Labor

The term "force account" refers to construction work the Agency may perform using its own forces. Examples may be mass transit, where a force account will be used to construct part of the work within their area of expertise. In this case, material, supplies and equipment are furnished by the Agency, and this work is not part of the contracted work. Force account labor may also be used as a result of an "emergency" situation or when force account construction is more practical and more cost effective than competitive bidding practices.

Prevailing Wages

The pay rates and cash equivalent of benefits as represented in union collective bargaining agreements with each trade in construction generally often set the "prevailing wage" for that trade. We have already discussed prevailing wages in the New York City labor market. In 2005, the prevailing wage of a construction laborer in Saginaw, Michigan was $35.25 per hour. The average wage for a non-union carpenter was $17.95 per hour. A union laborer earned $27.12 per hour, and a non-union laborer averaged $12 per hour. On a public job, the non-union laborer would be required to earn $27.12

per hour plus the cash equivalent of benefits paid to the union laborer.

The Davis Bacon Act

The Davis-Bacon Act requires that all contractors and subcontractors performing work on federally funded or assisted contracts must be paid not less than the prevailing wage rates and fringe benefits established for each construction trade. Wages for registered apprentices are lower than their journey level counterparts in a trade if they are in a U.S. Department of Labor registered apprenticeship training program. Employers who are covered under Davis-Bacon are required to post "Employee Rights under the Davis-Bacon Act" posters in visible locations. Contractors are required to maintain payroll and basic records of all laborers and mechanics during the course of the work, and maintain these records for three years after the job is completed. The records must indicate:

- Name, address and social security number of each employee

- Each employee work classification

- Hourly rates of pay and costs for fringe benefits or their cash equivalents

- Daily and weekly numbers of hours worked

- Deductions made and actual wages paid

- Approved apprenticeship training programs operating on the project

Little Davis-Bacon Laws

In addition to the federal Davis-Bacon Act, other jurisdictions have passed "Little Davis-Bacon Laws". For example, the Alaska Department of Labor and Workforce Development enforces that state's Little Davis-Bacon Act, which is intended by law to provide a level playing field for contractors to bid on public construction projects through minimum prevailing wage rates specific to that state. Otherwise, contractors who do not pay prevailing rates to their employees, when bidding public work, would most likely come in with the lowest bid, all other things being equal.

New York State's Little Davis-Bacon Act is contained in Section 220 of the Labor Law. The law parallels much of the Federal Davis-Bacon law, requiring all contractors and subcontractors engaged on public work projects to comply with wage schedules issued by the state's Labor Department, and these schedules must be made part of the contract between government entities and the Contractor. These requirements also flow down to subcontracts signed with the prime contractor.

Prevailing Wage Violations

In 2013, the California Labor Commissioner ordered an HVAC contractor to pay more than $960,000 in wages and fines for failure to pay ten workers the correct prevailing wage for work performed on a community college modernization project. Sheet metal workers were paid between $8.50 and $16 per hour when the rate should have been $55.06 per hour.

A New York contractor was arrested for failing to pay legally required wages to workers on a job at JFK International Airport for the Port Authority of NY and NJ. In this case, the company was a tile installation subcontractor who was paying tile setters wages ranging from $10 - $30 per hour, instead of the $70 per hour prevailing wage. To compound this non-compliance, the Contractor falsified certified payroll reports by showing that prevailing wages was being paid. Workers were paid the prevailing rate, and then were instructed to cash the checks at the Contractor's bank and kick back the majority of the cash to him.

In New York State, the Attorney General announced that two contractor firms owned by members of the same family agreed to pay more than $500,000 in restitution to workers for work performed for school and park construction projects with New York City agencies. Some of these workers were only earning a few dollars over minimum wage.

There are numerous other examples of similar violations in Chicago, Detroit and other locations in the United States. In these and other cases, depending on the extent to which employers seek to evade prevailing wage requirements, criminal charges can range from violations of Labor Law charges, to class C and D and E felonies and falsifying business records, resulting in fines, restitution and imprisonment.

Project Labor Agreements

A Project Labor Agreement (PLA) is an agreement that provides for the employment of labor union workers on a specific construction project. Before hiring begins for a project governed by a PLA, construction unions have the right to bargain to determine wages and fringe benefits for all of the employees who will be working on this particular project. The PLA will supersede any existing collective bargaining agreements because they are addressing the needs of a single particular project. PLAs have been used in private and publicly funded projects for years, and are actually authorized under the National Labor Relations Act. As PLAs have come into use more frequently on publicly funded projects, there has been much debate centering on whether a PLA discriminates against non-union contractors, and whether the intended reduction in costs and efficiency are actually occurring.

The Pro and Con Argument for Use of PLAs

The U.S. Chamber of Commerce and other groups have been active in their opposition of PLAs. They object to the fact that contractors are required to pay into union benefit plans and comply with union work rules, where they are not signatories to collective bargaining agreements, in order to work on a particularly project.

Opponents argue that PLA projects in the public sector add to costs because non-union contractors, who would normally bid with the intention of complying with prevailing wage without obligations to unions, will not bid a PLA project, reducing the number of bidders and driving up bid prices. They cite the "Big Dig" in Boston, a PLA project, as an example of where the PLA did not prevent huge cost overruns. Objections most frequently heard about using PLAs on public projects include the following:

- They increase costs by mandating union wages and work rules and inhibit competition

- Non union contractors may not bid because their members may be required to join a union if the Contractor wins the bid, or may not be able to hire their own workers if hiring is required through a union hall

- Are unnecessary because there are already existing prequalification procedures already in place to screen qualified contractors

- There is no evidence to support contentions that PLA projects are safer, more efficient or less costly

Opponents of PLAs question whether there is a legitimate reason in promoting public policy that, in their view, slows or reverses the decline of union workforce utilization, wages and benefits.

Many believe that prevailing wage laws are a means to aide unions in keeping member wages above what the market would normally require. Prevailing wages are in fact higher than those paid to non-union trades persons. As more non-union workers appear on construction contracts, it has been argued that PLAs are a way to neutralize the ability of nonunion contractors to compete for public work.

Many opponents believe that there are a number of nonunion contractors that are large enough to work on major public projects and they develop and retain their own workforce by offering health, retirement, vacation, training and other benefits. Once they sign onto a PLA project, workers are now coming through a union hiring hall and may not be part of the regular workforce of these nonunion companies. It has also been argued that nonunion skilled tradespersons often elect to work for nonunion companies because they do not want to pay union dues or be governed by union hiring rules, and can still secure good wages and benefits working for the nonunion contractor.

Those who argue for the implementation of PLAs include unions and some public policy makers. In 2013, President Barach Obama endorsed the use of PLAs on federal projects. Unions argue that PLAs provide job stability and prevent cost delays by providing uniform contract expiration dates, so that projects are not adversely impacted by the expiration of various collective bargaining agreements. They also believe that PLAs guarantee labor peace because of no-strike and no-lockout provisions. Advocates of PLAs believe that they guarantee a continuous source of highly qualified and trained workers who provide quality and work safely.

The advocates of PLAs believe that they:

- Provide uniform wages, benefits, pay, working conditions and work rules

- Provide contractors with a reliable source of qualified workers

- Enhance the probability of project completion on time and within budget

- With unions working under one contract, large scale projects are more manageable

- Promote recruitment and training of new workers through the use of apprenticeship and training programs for the project

In today's construction market, trade unions continue to be able to exercise power and influence in public construction, but as more and more contractors employ non-union labor, the result will be that clout of unions will decline, especially in their ability to set wages and control work rules. In the late 1940's construction workers who were union members reached 87 percent of all U.S. workers, and according to the Bureau of Labor Services, they were 15.5 percent nationally in 2009 but were earning 51.5 percent more than their non-union counterparts.

Chapter 6 References

The following sources were utilized in writing this chapter:

Kotler, Fred. "Project Labor Agreements in New York State II. In the Public Interest and of Proven Value. Cornell University. www.digitalcommons.lir.cornell.edu

Moran, John. Pros and Cons of Using Project Labor Agreements. 11/2/22011/ John Moran. OLR Research Report. www.cga.ct.gov/2011/rpt/2011-R-0360.htm

Tuerk, David. "Why Project Labor Agreements are not in the Public Interest." Journal. Vol. 30, No. 1, 2010

USDOL Website. Employment Law Guide www.dol.gov/compliance/guide/dbra.htm

CHAPTER 7
PROJECT CONTROLS
Cost and Schedule
Construction Estimates

Introduction

The **construction budget** and the **CPM project schedule** provide the baseline for tracking the project, to determine whether the project is running on time and within the budget. Prior to construction, a detailed final cost estimate serves as a control to measure costs. The budget may change due to circumstances that are either planned or unforeseen. The budget establishes project cost accounts for discrete activities that make up the total project. This allows for management of costs at the source activity that can cause overruns.

The inability of the project to be completed on time or within budget is among the risks faced by the Agency. Many things can happen that will increase the likelihood of risks. The Owner, designer, contractor and/or Construction Manager can each contribute to risk for numerous reasons. It is incumbent on the project management team to recognize the possibility of risk, identify risk and take decisive action to counteract or address them. A good construction schedule is the foundation of a successful construction project. Proper CPM scheduling reduces uncertainty for contractors and Owners and decreases the potential for financial losses associated with delays. It is a management tool to evaluate progress and to analyze the impact on going decisions will have on the overall construction project.

Schedule control allows the Agency's management team to identify and track the interrelationship of all activities, track the logical sequence of activities in preconstruction and construction phases of the project, and to identify deviations from the project plan.

The Project Budget

The *Budget* and *Cost Control* go hand in glove. Cost control on the project begins with the use of the construction budget plan and cash flow estimates as a baseline for monitoring costs. Schedules, actual progress of the work, and the achievement of project milestones are compared to the current project schedule, to monitor the progress of activities.

Just as the construction contract documents provide the baseline for quality of the work, the final cost estimate provides a baseline for financial performance. For a project to be under financial control, costs are within the detailed cost estimate.

The detailed final cost estimate prepared by the Agency, Architect / Engineer, or the Construction Manager is converted into a **project budget**, and this will be the guide for financial cost management for the duration of the project. As there may be many items of work in more complicated projects, expenses incurred are recorded in discrete job cost accounts that are linked back to the original cost estimate by category. This is the basic mechanism for cost control. Even if job cost accounts become divided into work elements, the budget can be configured in this manner to track costs.

Construction **cost accounts** are derived from work elements related to particular scheduled activities. Expenses are incurred during a project and are recorded in specific job cost accounts, which can be compared to original cost estimates in each category.

The construction estimate and the subsequent budget are mostly based on data for material quantities and labor within each job account. Thus, actual hours of work by job classification, and actual materials and equipment can be compared to the budget. Cost savings or overruns for particular items are easily identified. Where there are cost overruns, the portents for these are changes in unit prices, labor productivity, or the amount of material and equipment actually used.

We will illustrate cost accounts by looking at a simple work item, "Clearing and Preparing the Site". If we do not break down this general category, it becomes more difficult to estimate and track the costs associated with this activity. If, however, we break this into subtasks, we can very clearly identify costs for each sub-activity and control cost at the sub-activity level:

Example of a Project Cost Account	
101	Clearing and Preparing Site
102	Substructure
102.1	Excavating and Shoring
102.2	Piles
102.3	Concrete
102.31	Mixing and Placing Material
102.32	Formwork
102.33	Reinforcing

All projects have a need for contingencies for unforeseen events. There are costs that cannot be known at the time of budget preparation, but can be budgeted through contingencies. These can be refined later. Therefore the budget should include a contingency allowance which should also be reflected in the project budget. All significant programmatic and Owner controlled scope changes that occur during the design or construction phase include the following:

- Design Changes - During the design phase, all changes are scope changes and should not be funded using a project contingency.
- Construction Changes - Changes relating to unforeseen conditions, designer errors and omissions, code compliance, allowance overages, and time-related expenses deemed acceptable by the Owner.
- Owner / Agency Controlled Changes - Changes proposed by contractors and/or Project Managers as new construction-related ideas and opportunities arise that reduce costs or improve outcomes such as new materials and processes.

- Programmatic Changes - Scope increase to re-program the space and/or systems that require additional funding.

On longer term projects, another issue that arises is the costs associated with inflation. Inflation costs need to be factored into the project budget, either as a lump sum or a percentage, and then allocated to individual cost items.

Risk Factors in Construction

The **risk** to your construction project is that there is a danger of damage, loss or injury. The inability for the project to be completed on time and/or within budget are risks of construction. Many things can happen during the project cycle that increases the likelihood for risk. The Owner, designer and contractor can all be subject to construction project pitfalls that increase risk.

Owner / Agency:
- Funding issues
- Deficient construction contract documents
- Furnished materials not available
- Major changes in requirements
- Failure to make progress payments
- Interference

Designer
- Deficient plans and specifications
- Shop drawing and submittal review and approval
- Improper or delayed change orders
- Failure to coordinate between Architect / Engineer

Contractor
- Slow to mobilize
- Failure to properly staff the project
- Inadequate equipment
- Failure to coordinate
- Inadequate project management

- Non compliance with contract quality requirements

Construction Manager
- Inadequate design and constructability review
- Inadequate Project Management
- Delays in Coordinating Change Orders
- Slow Payment Processing
- Interference with Contractors

Risk Factors that Can Imperil Construction

Funding Issues

In the private sector, adequate funding of projects is becoming a more difficult task. Lenders are enforcing much more stringent guidelines for construction owners, and bankers are far more selective in terms of the types of projects they are willing to fund.

The case is a little different in the public sector. Generally, projects do not move forward until funds have been appropriated and budgeted, and allocated to the public agency. However, in the early part of the 21st Century, many very large scale projects that have started are not fully funded, and may never be fully funded, even though they are in progress. Some have even been abandoned after starting. On other public projects, changes brought on for various reasons cause the current budget to be exceeded, and funding may not be available for the changes.

Owner Furnished Materials

Unique projects may require agencies to procure their own equipment, particularly for project s such as research facilities, hospitals and educational facilities. Owners need to be able to understand the Contractor's material management plans for timely installation.

Major Scope Changes

The Agency must define the scope of the project, and it is expected that in the conceptual phase, and even as the design progresses beyond conceptual, the scope will change. However, the further along we are in the project cycle, the more likely these changes will cause hardships. Changes may arise because the Owner's desires have changed, or because of design reviews, constructability issues, value engineering considerations, field conditions, safety issues, operation and management concerns.

Defective Plans and Specifications

Errors and omissions in the design documents always require modifications later on in the project that may not have been foreseen.

Slow to Mobilize

Poor planning or a lack of resources causes delays in mobilization by the Contractor. In order for mobilization to happen, the Contractor needs to have sufficient labor, equipment and materials required for the sequence of work that is being kicked off.

Failure to Allocate Resources

The Contractor is profit driven and does not want to commit more manpower and equipment than is absolutely necessary. Cash flow needs are increased with more commitment of resources. The key is for the Contractor to be able to manage with limited amounts of manpower and equipment and to bring in more resources precisely when they are needed as the activity builds. Without the right mix of people, equipment and materials on site, risk factors increase.

Inadequate Project Management Controls

The lack of cost management systems and reporting, confusion about the authority to make decisions, lack of integrated planning, lack of communication, and the inability to take decisive action when needed all add to project risk.

Other Factors

Failure to properly define the project scope in enough detail for appropriate decisions concerning the schedule, estimates and allocation of resources, poses more risks for the project. Unrealistic schedules and underestimated costs based on optimistic predictions causes burdens and missed milestone dates.

Identifying Areas of Risk in Construction

Timing factors put projects at higher risk when the project is of short term duration, fast tracked. Risk factors are more moderate for projects that will take months or years.

The nature of the project also poses risk based on the type of construction, project size, complexity, location, and the status of the plans and specifications. State of the art projects, large rehabilitation projects, and projects in new geographic or more remote areas pose a higher risk factor.

The approval process is another risk factor. All construction projects have various levels of approval that must be obtained before construction starts. These can include environmental approvals, historic preservation, community standards that are stringent, and other factors.

The approval process can cause time delays and overruns. Public perception of projects, especially those deemed controversial, encounter approval processes that may be lengthy, such as the construction of a nuclear power plant, highways that encroach wetlands, because of the perceived impact on the community.

The type of experience of the Owner or agency impacts risk. An owner organization that is inexperienced in construction, or does not engage qualified design and construction management professionals create more risk on the project. Risks result from required changes, sufficient funding, scope changes, etc. The type of project delivery also impacts risk. Lump sum and fixed price contracts are less risky than fast track cost plus type contracts.

Weak project management controls contribute to risk. Schedule and cost control systems that are linked together by a cost loaded schedule is a better management tool for the management of risk.

Minimizing Risk

Risk is first minimized in the planning phase of a project. Claims arise from ambiguity in the construction contract documents, errors and omissions, underestimated or overstated quantities, design changes, late precedence work by others, work access constraints, late Owner furnished materials and equipment.

Strong management systems include comprehensive schedules. The requirements for a network scheduling CPM type systems should be a requirement of the contract. Contractors selected by the Agency should have the management capability to operate under these and other management systems.

Proper scoping of the work and its risk and budgeting and cost management systems are required to manage performance of the job. Contractors must have cost accounting systems and procedures that permit separate tracking of costs for any work outside of the scope of the contract.

Certain articles of the contract need to clearly specify all rights and obligations of the parties. Typically, the following articles usually come into play in regard to claims and disputes: changes, changed conditions, variations in quantities for unit cost, termination for default, damages for delay, time extensions, and escalation of labor or material.

Minimizing risk is shared by all parties to your contract. Your project has a degree of uncertainty built into it. Risk is a fact of construction and can arise with every decision made on the project. By understanding risk factors and how to mange them, potential risk can be avoided or abated.

Project Cost Control

Project Cost Control refers to different tasks that are performed to control the cost of your project. These include:

- Actions taken in pre-construction, including adequate constructability reviews to minimize unexpected costs
- Developing the construction cost cash flow plan

- Monitoring cost performance during the construction phase to identify deviations from the project budget and understand why these are occurring, and reacting to these indicators to provide corrective action
- Ensuring that all approved changes are recorded accurately in the cost
- Communicating proposed and authorized changes to stakeholders.
- Acting to bring costs within acceptable budget limits.
- Baseline and preventing incorrect, inappropriate and/or unauthorized changes from being included in the cost baseline.

The purpose of project cost control is to manage risk. Risk is the possibility that the project will not meet planned goals for cost or time. The result are project cost overruns and late project delivery. The project cost control system seeks to raise the red flags of potential risk. The system will allow for the comparison of planned vs. actual labor and material output translating to actual cost.

There are various tools that are used by Project Managers to determine whether a project is on target to meet its budget and schedule. These include: Critical Path Method Scheduling (CPM), Work Breakdown Structure (WBS), and Earned Value Management (EVM).

Work Breakdown Structure

CPM and WBS are very much intertwined. The WBS enables the Construction Manager to manage time and money on your project because it provides a link between the tasks associated with a specific activity and the planned budget and schedule for that activity.

The project is the sum total of thousands of discrete activities that, when added together, equal to the tasks required to build a project. Each of these discrete activities bears on the schedule and the budget. To the extent that project activities can be broken down to its various elements, project performance for cost and schedule becomes easier to identify, down to the details of the project that are contributing to meeting the budget and the schedule. The WBS uses a hierarchical structure for project management. The first two levels of the WBS define a set of planned outcomes that equal 100% of the project scope. At each subsequent level, activities are broken down into sub scopes and the activities within the sub scope equal 100 percent of the activity at the subsequent level.

There are four elements in each WBS element. Each WBS element contains the scope of work, including deliverables, the beginning and end date for the scope of work, the budget for the scope of work, and the identity of responsibility for the scope of work. By breaking down the project into WBS elements, the Construction Manager can look at a complex project and dissect it into identifiable, manageable parts. The WBS is developed for each construction work package.

Below is a simplified example of WBS Breakdown for a new building. The major tasks are construction of the substructure, superstructure, envelope, and interior finishes, as shown in the figure below:

NEW BUILDING			
A Substructure	B Superstructure	C Envelope	D Interior
Concrete	Roof Deck	Roofing	MEP Systems
Excavation	Siding	Windows	Interior Finishes

Using **WBS "A"** for Substructure in the above example, we can go to the sub-element "concrete" and we review the resources, units of measurement, outputs, and quantities and link these back to the CPM schedule and the project budget. Here is an example of how this is done. We will breakout concrete for grade beam installation, a sub element of the concrete activity:

A / Concrete: Grade beam Installation

Activity	Resources	Units	Output per Day	Total	Duration in Days
Grade beam A-1	Concrete (Material)	CY	300	3,000	10
Grade beam A-1	Trade Labor	Hour	100	1,000	10

We have isolated one of the elements of the construction of the substructure. We have broken substructure into two activities comprising the substructure, concrete and excavation. We have further divided tasks for concrete and have illustrated one discrete element, installation of grade beam.

The cost and time associated with this activity is based on the installation of material and the labor required for its installation. The next step, which is illustrated below, will tie the budget into this WBS example:

Activity	Resource	Unit	Cost Per Unit	Total Units	Budget
Grade beam A-1	Concrete (Material)	CY	$100	3,000	$300,000
Grade beam A-1	Trade Labor	Hsr	$40	80	$3,200
BUDGET FOR GRADEBEAM WBS					**$303,200**

We have now successfully isolated the time and budget associated with this aspect of the construction of the substructure. This process is completed for all WBS items in the budget, and this will give you an idea of how the budget and schedule is monitored and controlled using the WBS in conjunction with the baseline budget and CMP schedule.

Earned Value Management

Another cost and schedule control management tool is Earned Value Management (EVM). This is a management system that is used in general project management, including construction. Earned value management combines schedule and cost performance in order to measure whether value on the project is being achieved based on costs and schedule progress in a given point in time. EVM is used to identify **scope creep**, where unplanned and uncontrolled changes in scope occur. EVM helps to identify "red flags" for performance problems as it measures project scope, schedule and cost.

Scheduling software programs like Primavera integrate the schedule with budget and cost data to generate EVM reports. A baseline CPM schedule is used with cost/resource loading. These include manpower hours, construction equipment, cost, and materials. In this process, the following is determined:

- The budgeted cost of work that is scheduled
- The actual cost of work performed
- Actual work performed at the budgeted cost

Schedule Control

The Agency needs to have the project delivered within a specific time period, and the facility needs to be turned over for utilization by the Owner. By establishing the schedule, the parameters and maximum time allowed for completion of the project are established.

The project has a deadline for completion, and the Agency's contracts will reference compliance with the approved schedule. A delay in construction translates to additional costs incurred because of a late facility being delivered. Schedule control is interrelated to cost control. In cost control, we are comparing actual to budget costs. In schedule control, we are comparing actual activity duration to expected or scheduled durations. As in cost control, there are forecasting methods used to estimate time for completion of project activities. In its simplest form, the duration of time equals the amount of work multiplied by productivity.

The Construction Manager must work with the Contractor to determine all means and methods to achieve this date. This may mean expediting the work with multiple shifts or other fast tracking methods. There should be a liquidated damages provision in the contract that sets a daily charge to the Contractor to compensate the Agency for costs incurred when the facility cannot be used. This is the basis for liquidated damages, not as a penalty for being late, but compensation for costs incurred by the Agency for late delivery.

Observations of work completed are provided by the Construction Manager or design team. Once we know the estimate of work complete and time already expended on an activity, the deviations from the duration contained in the original schedule can be estimated.

The Agency's date for delivery may not reflect the actual time needed using normal practices for the construction of the project, but the Agency's need trumps all else. If you need to have a school ready in

August because they are accepting students at the end of that month, there is no flexibility on the delivery of the school. If the construction can be completed in the least amount of time, the Contractor's jobsite overhead will be reduced, and other jobs can be pursued. The Contractor is motivated to complete the project in the shortest amount of time without increasing cost with overtime and other lost productivity. In this regard, the Construction Manager and the Contractor need to carefully plan construction sequencing and the realistic amount of time needed for various activities. The project plan for completing on time involves the following considerations:

- Activities and duration of activities on the project
- Sequencing of work and coordination of trades dependent on each other to proceed
- Equipment requirements
- Delivery dates for long lead items and the delivery of materials
- Crew sizes and manpower needed
- Availability of subcontractors to perform when needed
- Anticipating for seasonal weather conditions, and lost days for weather

Each of the activities of a project needs to be identified in order to prepare a realistic project schedule. The sequence of activities needs to be established, and the duration of time required for these activities needs to be known. The plan for the project determines the sequence of activities. Sequence is based on quality considerations, such as when to pour concrete, and / or dependency on preceding activities. The purpose of schedule control is to confirm the viability of the original plan, determining and implementing appropriate action where performance is deviating form the plan, and in ensuring commitment of all parties to meet the plan by complying with the schedule. The duration of an activity must be accurately predicted. It is relative to the amount of labor hours required, the quantity of work to be accomplished, weather concerns, delivery of all items when needed, and subcontractor involvement.

The project schedule is based on the project plan, and is a graphical depiction of the plan. The schedule becomes a tool to communicate the project plan among the project stakeholders. These days, scheduling software produces graphs and reports. The Agency's primary interests are:

- Completion dates
- Project milestones for partial completion
- Dates and relationship of Owner furnished items and separate contracts
- Current activities in progress
- Schedule for Owner provided services, as applicable

The Architect is interested in knowing the same things as the Agency, but also is focused on the status of problem areas and projected changes, relationship of submittal review to the schedule, and the schedule for inspection or observation involving the Architect.

In analyzing a project schedule, it is important to understand the concept of "float". Float is like a contingency of additional time, meaning that an activity time for completion has some flexibility, as opposed to activities that are on a critical path. A critical path activity that is delayed will cause a project delay, and this is a serious scheduling issue.

By using the schedule as a management tool, you are better able to monitor timely completion of work and determine if there is adequate labor, materials and equipment at the site, adequate supervision, orderly sequence of work and coordination by trade.

There are different schedule types and uses. They vary based on the complexity of the project and levels of detail in the project. The simplest schedule is a bar chart. A listing of activities is placed in a column on the left side of the chart, and a calendar shows the duration of the activity extended for the duration of the project. The bar chart is easy to understand, shows time frames for major activities, and can incorporate schedule of values and other payment information. However, on other than very simple projects, it does not provide enough detail to be a useful management tool. It does not show relationships of activities.

Critical Path Method (CPM)

The **Critical Path Method (CPM)** is computer generated, and shows an activity's start and completion points, duration, dependencies on previous activities, and relationships with future activities. Each activity references all relationships and is shown on the project calendar. As the project progresses, updated information is added to each activity's information and an updated schedule is generated.

The CPM builds the model for the project, showing all activities required to complete the project within a work breakdown structure. It shows the time that each activity is planned to require for completion, and the dependencies between these activities.

The CPM then calculates the path of planned activities from the start to the finish of the project. It will show the earliest and latest that each activity can start and finish without extending the time of the project. It shows which activities are critical (follow the longest path) and which can be delayed (total float) without delaying the project. The critical path is the calculated path for the project that takes into consideration the dependency on activities that must precede subsequent activity in order for the project to progress. The predecessors or activities that come before are analyzed. The longest duration of a predecessor activity establishes the start date of the activity in the critical path. Any change to an activity on the critical path directly affects the completion of the project. A project can have several, parallel, near critical paths. An additional parallel path through the network with the total durations shorter than the critical path is called a sub-critical or non-critical path.

Activities not on a critical path have a **float**. This term refers to a period of time in addition to the activity's duration, prior to the start of the next, or successor activity. The float allows some flexibility of time with non critical items, and provides flexibility in duration and the actual start of an item. Thus if there is a three days float for an item with an early start date of September 1, the time can start anywhere between September 1st and September 3rd.

By preparing and analyzing the schedule, the Construction Manager and contractor can plan the project by prioritizing activities for the effective management of project completion, and to shorten the planned critical path of a project by fine tuning critical path activities, by **"fast tracking"**, such as by performing more activities in parallel, and/or by **"crashing the critical path"**, which simply means to shorten the durations of critical path activities by adding resources.

Cost and schedule monitoring must happen continuously. As changes occur or discrepancies between planned and actual performance are identified, red flags signal corrective action and the modification of schedules and cost estimates. Without updating and adjustment of activity durations and budgets, the depiction of the project is no longer realistic or accurate without changing the baselines for budget and time. Construction projects normally involve numerous activities which are closely related, one affecting the other. Without updating, project schedules will continue to slip as the project progresses. The expected duration or estimate of activities needs to be updated based on real time conditions and activities. The estimated resources necessary for each activity, including manpower, equipment and materials need to be modified. Scheduling software makes it relatively easy to make these adjustments.

Construction Estimating

A **construction estimate** is a calculation of quantities for work scope items, and the likely cost to perform the cost of the work. The estimated cost should be fairly close to actual cost, providing that estimating methods and a correct understanding of the scope of work are applied. If your project is not estimated properly it could result in the cancelation of the project, or its postponement due to appropriation and funding issues.

Estimating is critical to your project. It is intended to provide the Agency with a reasonably accurate parameter of cost, and is critical in determining what can be accomplished with funding that is available.

The elements that factor into estimates are: (a) the estimate of materials; (b). the estimate of labor; (c) the estimate of equipment required to install the work; and (d) the estimate of time required to complete an item of work.

Types of Estimates

There are different categories of estimates. Generally, these are referred to **approximate estimates, and detailed estimates**. An approximate estimate is really a rough estimate of cost to get a "ball park" idea of cost. A detailed estimate of the cost of your project is prepared by determining quantities and costs for all work items that will be provided by the Contractor for the satisfactory completion of all work. A detailed cost estimate is prepared based on a unit quantities method and a total quantities method.

To establish a budget and request the appropriation of funding for the Agency's project, a design estimate is used. As the project progresses toward bidding, the construction cost estimates are first implemented in the design phase. The **design estimate** may take the form of: order of magnitude estimates, preliminary or conceptual estimates, and detailed estimates. The amount of design information needed increases in order for each of these estimates to be completed. The most detailed estimate in this phase is based on highly progressed plans and specifications.

The Construction Manager will prepare a **control estimate** that in many ways parallels the Contractor's bid. This will include the estimate of direct construction costs of labor and material plus the markup to cover overhead and profit.

The Contractor, in submitting the bid, has also estimated these costs, and has utilized subcontractor quotations, quantity takeoffs, and intended means and methods to construct. The Construction Manager has also considered these, and has sourced the market for pricing as well, in an attempt to accurately estimate realistic costs, so that there is a control on the bids received, to determine that they are reasonable given market conditions for labor, material, and equipment.

Design Estimates

In the planning and design stages, estimates are prepared as the design progresses. In the very early part of the project, this may be an **order of magnitude estimate**, before any design has actually begun. It relies on historical data from similarly constructed facilities built in the recent past, and the experience of the estimator with similar projects.

A *preliminary estimate* or *conceptual estimate* uses design information available in the conceptual design stage of the project. Basic design assumptions are known based on schematics and design report recommendations to the Agency.

The *detailed estimate* will be prepared when the scope of work is clearly defined, and detailed design is underway and sufficiently detailed to identify essential features of the project.

The *final estimate* (sometimes called the engineer's estimate) is based on the completed plans and specifications that will be incorporated into the Agency's bidding documents. The level of detail will mirror tasks to be performed by the Contractor.

The following illustrates the different estimates prepared in design for a new bridge over water:

- A conceptual estimate is made for each alternative bridge type. Perhaps it will be a beam bridge, truss bridge or arch bridge
- The order of magnitude estimate will be applied to each bridge type of cost comparison purposes
- Once the actual bridge type is selected, the preliminary estimate will be made based on the schematic layout of the bridge based on details in the conceptual design stage
- Once design has progresses sufficiently, more details essential to the construction process that will be required are known
- At this point, a detailed estimate can be prepared because key elements of the bridge project are now known, and the scope of the work is more detailed
- At the completion of plans and specifications, the final or engineer's estimate is made based on items and quantities of work

Contractor Bid Estimates

The effort put into the Contractor's bid estimate is based on the level of desire the Contractor has to win the job. Some contractors may decide that they are too busy but will submit a "courtesy" bid. Courtesy bids are bid amounts that are too high and are not likely to be accepted by the Agency. A contractor may submit this type of bid because he wants to maintain a relationship with the Agency and keep the firm on the radar. The Contractor is also aware that the

Agency needs to receive a certain number of bids because of procurement requirements.

A serious bidder who wants the work will put a great level of effort into the bid. Some contractors have comprehensive procedures for bidding, maintaining experiential cost data for the market they are bidding in. They may have a full time estimator or estimating department. They will also obtain prices from subcontractors who will perform work that the general contractor will not self perform. At the other end of the spectrum, a general contractor may not have a full time estimator, or may rely on bid estimates from the subcontractors, shifting the burden of the estimate to the subs.

If the general contractor plans to self perform the work, or most of it, the basis of the bid estimate will be quantity takeoffs from the plans that were provided in the bid documents. The Contractor may refer to published cost data or research costs directly based on labor, material and equipment needed to perform the work.

Control Estimates

The control estimate provides the Agency with a baseline for cost control. As the work progresses, the project budget must be revised periodically to reflect the estimated cost to completion. A revised estimated cost is necessary as a result of change orders or overruns and under runs. The budgeted cost requires periodic update to reflect estimated cost to completion and to ensure adequate funding for the completion of the project.

Estimating Methods

Preparing cost estimates requires the use of historical data on construction costs. **Historical cost data** must relate to means, methods and processes relevant to your project in order to be useful. Historical data requires updates because of changes that occur over time. The format of cost data, such as unit costs for various items, should be organized based on contract quantities for payment to the Contractor.

There are data base software programs for Construction Specifications Institute (CSI) MasterFormat divisions that are accepted across the construction industry. MasterFormat is a master list of numbers and titles for use with construction requirements, products, and activities by sequence. The CSI MasterFormat provides an organization and structure for construction work activities into 16 divisions.

The **work breakdown structure** as previously discussed, provides for a consistent format in developing the estimate. It provides an ordered sequence for summarizing information in order to present quantitative data.

The estimator creates the work breakdown structure by identifying major deliverables and dividing these into small systems and sub deliverables. These are then further broken down as required. At this level, specific work packages required to produce the sub-deliverable are identified and grouped together.

At the most detailed level of activity, a crew is able to perform the work. The estimator prepares a task description by defining the level of effort to construct the work item. Another method to provide a detailed task by task estimated is known as **parametric estimates**. In this process, various factors are used to come up with the estimate, including historical data, construction practices, and construction methodology. This type of estimate is useful when design details are not available. It is based on average costs for similar projects and coming up with an estimated square foot cost. This is applied to estimated quantities.

Published Cost Data

Construction **cost data** are published in various forms by several organizations, and these are used as references for cost comparisons. These include catalogs of data from vendors relating to their building products. One such type of publication is the *Sweets' Catalog* published by McGraw-Hill Information Systems Company.

Commercial cost reference manuals are published for estimating guides. An example is the *Building Construction Cost Data* published annually by R.S. Means Company, Inc. This contains unit prices on building construction items.

Unit Quantity Method

The *Unit Quantity Method* divides the work into many different items. A unit of measurement is determined. The total quantity of work under each item is provided for based on the unit of measurement used for payment. The total cost (which includes cost of materials, labor, plant, overhead and profit) will be shown as the unit cost for the item and then multiplied by the quantities for that item. The total quantities of each kind or class of material or labor are found and multiplied by their individual unit cost. Similarly, the cost of plant, overhead expenses and profit are determined. The costs of all the five sub-heads are summed up to give the estimated cost of the item of work.

Cost Estimating Basics

Accuracy and completeness are critical in developing the cost estimate. Accurate estimating establishes financial cost control parameters. The Agency needs to have confidence in the estimate. A thorough review of the contract documents for ambiguity, clarity of scope, conflicting requirements in the specifications, and risk factors.

All construction cost estimates should have an independent review, either by other estimators, the Construction Manager's estimating department or independent cost estimating services. The review tests the validity of assumptions in the estimate.

The estimate consists of work / task elements, quantity of work required by task, cost for each task quantity, and time to complete the task.

The construction documents are thoroughly reviewed, including supplemental and general conditions, any environmental impact statements applicable to the project, and other requirements that will increase costs.

The estimator must be able to fully understand the scope of work and the conditions under which the construction will be built by reviewing the drawings, specifications, geotechnical reports and other project documentation.

The sequence of work must be formulated for the estimate, as this affects the cost estimating process.

The quantity takeoff is based on the analysis of scope, the work breakdown structure methodology discussed above, and the quantification of each task. Quantities need to be shown as a standard unit of measurement and should be consistent with design units, such as the English or Metric system. The detail to which quantities are developed for each task has a direct relationship to the level of design detail for the task available for the estimate.

Types of Costs

Direct Costs are costs that can be attributed to a single task of work. These costs are attributed to the cost of construction crews performing the task, with specific materials for that task. The use of a subcontractor should be considered as part of the direct cost.

Indirect Costs are costs that can not be directly attributed to a specific task in the construction. These include costs for the bond, overhead, and profit factor. *Escalation* and *contingencies* are also added to the cost estimate.

Productivity

Productivity is the measurement of a unit of work done and the unit of time that it is completed. The unit of work done can include the volume of material moved, the number of pieces of piping that is cut, or other measurements of production. The unit of time is a minute, an hour, a shift, a day, or other duration chosen to measure time for work accomplished.

The **production rate** measures work done in relation to the time required to perform the work. The formula is: *Production rate = Work Done / Unit of Time.*

Productivity is obviously important to the development of the estimate because it is the output per labor hour. A large part of the cost is labor, and the quantity of labor hours in performing a task in labor hours are a key to the estimate. **Labor productivity** is associated with units of production by labor in a given time period. Thus, on highway project, the cubic yards of concrete place per hour or miles of highway per hour measures labor productivity by linking labor to the value of construction for the material being place per labor hour.

In considering production rates in developing an estimate, the estimator must consider job factors and site conditions likely for the project being estimated. These factors may include:

- Experience and capability of project participants in this type of project

- Size and complexity of the project
- Availability of materials and equipment
- Climate
- Geographic location and topographic conditions
- Quality of job supervision and correct sequencing of work
- Repetition of tasks vs. new tasks
- Labor agreements and trade practices

Construction Plant and Equipment

Construction plant is denied as concrete batch plants, aggregate processing plants and other processing plants that are erected in place at the job site. Equipment includes all tools and heavy machinery, including cranes, backhoes and trucks.

In developing the estimate, the estimator will figure in costs for equipment anticipated for the construction project. Considerations for identifying equipment for the estimate include the production rate and schedule, availability of equipment, distances materials must be moved on site, steepness of grade, weather conditions, the cost of mobilization and demobilization, and restrictions on the use of equipment on the site.

Mobilization and Demobilization

Mobilization and demobilization costs must be included in the detailed estimate. Mobilization refers to all activities and cost for transportation of personnel, equipment, supplies and materials to the site, the establishment of field offices and other on site facilities necessary for contractor operations. Demobilization costs include costs for all activities including transportation of personnel, equipment and supplies/materials not used in the Contract, including the disassembly, removal and site cleanup of any offices, buildings or other facilities assembled on the site for the Contract.

Permanent Materials and Supplies

Permanent materials are those materials that are physically installed on the project and become part of the permanent structure. Supplies are used in construction, but do not become part of the physical structure, but are used to facilitate installation. In estimating, both are categorized as materials. Pricing for materials and supplies can be obtained from quotations from suppliers and manufacturers, from historical data and from catalogs. As prices are received, their reasonableness needs to be considered by the estimator before using this data in the estimate. The estimator will take into consideration quantity discounts, inflation and anything else that will affect the cost. An estimator uses *forward pricing* for work that will be in advance of the estimate to the degree that the prices need to be escalated.

Cost of Subcontractors

Many times, a general contractor prefers to have specialty work performed by others. Work such as plumbing, heating, ventilation, air conditioning, electrical, roofing, and special architectural finishes are subbed out.

In preparing the estimate, the estimator will determine work that is likely to be subcontracted out. The subcontractor's costs for labor, materials, overhead, profit, supplies, equipment, second tier subcontracts, etc. are considered to be direct costs to the prime contractor.

Overhead Costs

There are costs that cannot be allocated to a single task of construction work, and these costs are called overhead costs.

Overhead includes job office overhead, also called general conditions or field office overhead, and overhead for the home office, often called general and administrative (G&A) overhead.

The estimator must take care not to carry overlapping costs between these two types of overhead. The following indicates the cost factors that go into the computation of each type of overhead category.

Job Office Overhead	General and Admin. Overhead
• Project supervision	• Main office building
• Field office personnel	• Furniture and Equipment
• Drawings	• Home office utilities
• Temporary facilities	• General communications
• Preparatory work	• Travel
• Laboratory testing	• Supplies
• Telephone and communications	• Corporate Vehicles
	• General business insurance
• Permits and licenses	• Taxes

- Insurance for project
- Quality control
- Job site facilities
- Administration

Estimates are only as good as the experience of the estimator and the data input for the estimate. So, what makes a "good" estimate?

- **Clear identification of task.** The estimator must be provided with or have a clear project scope, ground rules, and construction means and methods, The estimate's constraints and conditions must be clearly identified to ensure the preparation of a good estimate.

- **Participation of the stakeholders.** In order to garner the information needed, consultation with project participants is required for their input.

- **Use of Valid Data.** There are many sources of data that can be used for the estimate. Data should be independently verified for accuracy, completeness, and reliability. Relevant, historical data can be used from similar projects or system components can be project costs of the new project and new systems. The historical data should be directly related to the requirements.

- **Work Breakdown Structure.** A standard work breakdown structure, as detailed as possible, will be used to refine the cost estimate. The standardized structure helps ensure that no portions of the estimate are left out, and facilitates comparisons with other similar project.

- **Escalation for Inflation.** The estimator should ensure that economic changes, such as inflation, are properly and realistically reflected in the life-cycle cost estimate.

- **Independent review of estimates.** Conducting an independent review of an estimate is crucial to establishing confidence in the estimate. The independent reviewer should verify, modify, and correct an estimate, as required.

- **Revision of estimates for significant program.** Estimates should be updated to reflect changes in requirements.

Chapter 7 References

The following sources were utilized in writing this chapter:

Baker, S. "Critical Path Method (CPM)" *University of South Carolina*, Health Services Policy and Management Courses Retrieved from: http://hspm.sph.sc.edu/COURSES/J716/CPM/CPM.html

Caletka, A. *Managing Construction Projects. Have You Taken Your Project's Pulse Lately? Project Health Checks.* May 13, 2009. Retrieved from: http://www.greyhawk.com/news/technical/Project.Health.Check-Caletka.pdf Hendrikson

Hendrikson, C. Fundamental Concepts for Owners, Engineers, Architects and Builders. World Wide Web Publication, 2000. Carnegie Mellon University. Retrieved from: http://pmbook.ce.cmu.edu/

Sweets Network of Building Products
http://products.construction.com/TopSearches

The R.S. Means Cost Data Book.
http://rsmeans.reedconstructiondata.com/60011.aspx

CHAPTER 8
Construction Manager
Agent of the Agency

What to Expect From the Construction Manager

The Agency has a project to build. To accomplish this, definable tasks must be accomplished to meet the objective of constructing the project. What are some of these?

- Complete the project within a specified time frame. Projects running past the delivery date blow the budget and may wreak havoc on operations due to late delivery
- Complete the project with the quality intended, with regard to material and equipment, workmanship, and integration of all components into a complete working facility
- Assure that project costs are not exceeded. Cost control of a project indicates a high level of productivity
- Run a safe project
- Ensure that the client that the Agency is building for, including itself, is satisfied by providing communication, attention to detail, coordination, and completion of the physical project as expected and when expected
- Effective management of contractors and subcontractors at the site

Our discussion here focuses on the Construction Manager as the Agent to the Owner / agency, because it is the most common form of CM utilization by public agencies. The construction management team brought to the project as your agent should be expected to provide the following attributes:

- Project Leadership
- Problem Solving
- Quality Management
- Safety Management

Project Leadership

Project leadership starts with the Agency. The vision for the entire project and what needs to be accomplished must be clearly communicated to the Construction Manager and the design team. The Construction Manager must be able to translate the Agency's vision into a viable plan for achieving the completed project by exercising **project leadership**. The Construction Manager must ensure that the project meets the budget through cost management system assessment and reporting to the Agency. The Construction Manager must develop a positive working relationship with the constructors of the project – general contractors, prime subcontractors and subcontractors. At the same time, positive and constructive relationships must also be maintained with the design team.

The Construction Manager must have a feel for what the trades are capable of, and to know what is necessary to increase productivity through motivation or implementing remedial actions to meet goals.

Problem Solving

Problems on a construction project can arrive fast and furiously. A competent Construction Manager may see the problems coming and take steps to prevent them or plan to deal with them proactively. Delays in solving problems cause more problems. It's like the noise you hear in your car when you are driving. It never goes away, and the problem gets worse if it isn't attended to.

Problem solving is not easy, and that is why you are paying the construction management firm so much tax payer money. Problems are complex, may involve several trades, subcontractors and suppliers. Each situation needs to be assessed and a decision needs to be made that will be least harmful or unfavorable to the project. In solving problems, the Construction Manager needs to consider:

- The full impact on the project participants and stakeholders
- Cost impact and responsibility for the cost
- Time impact and the appropriateness of time extensions and compensation
- Strategic solution, considering crews, equipment and materials, project progress, the environment of the project, and agency needs
- Conflict resolution between project participants

Quality Management

The Construction Manager will be expected to make substantial effort to assure quality on the project. **Quality** means that the expected level of material, workmanship and constructed facility meets the satisfaction of the Agency by complying with the plans, specifications, and design intent that was approved by the Agency.

On different levels, this means that each contractor has a quality assurance and quality control program to the satisfaction of the Construction Manager. It means that:

- Design and constructability reviews in preconstruction resulted in a set of construction documents that are detailed, clear and unambiguous
- The Architect/Engineer is promptly reviewing submittals before work begins, and that the Construction Manager is tracking these
- There is a testing program in place for materials and building systems
- There is daily inspection of work for construction document compliance, and that there is a running punchlist of items being corrected long before the end of the project
- All warranties and guarantees are received and in effect, and all materials and equipment have been installed as required by manufacturer's specifications

Safety Management

In the United States, the burden of safety falls on the general contractor and subcontractors. The Contractor is motivated to run a safe contract because savings can be realized in workers compensation premiums and insurance premiums by having a good Experience Modification Rating (EMR). The EMR measures worker compensation claims. Even with a good EMR, this does not mean that boneheaded, flagrant disregard for safety doesn't happen every day on country sites all over the country. The goal of safety management is to prevent accidents from happening. There are some agencies that do not empower the Construction Manager to be proactive in safety. This is a mistake. The Construction Manager should not only be empowered to stop any operation that is unsafe, but to demand that each contractor have a safety representative on site at all times, and an approved safety management plan. Depending on complexity and inherent risks to health and safety, the Agency may consider paying an additional fee to the Construction Manager to bring in safety managers to perform periodic safety reviews and audits.

Nuts and Bolts of Construction Management

Now let's get into some of the nuts and bolts of construction management services that you are entitled to receive and should receive from the Construction Manager. Once again, it is the job of the Construction Manager to complete the project on time, at or under budget, safety, and in a manner that meets the quality expectations of the Agency / Owner. The Construction Manager is your quarterback in a sense, the focal point of the project, responsible for coordinating project activities, sequencing work, monthly pay estimates, change orders, and complete project documentation. The Contractor is responsible for quality, ensuring that all materials have been properly installed as per the design intent and the construction contract documents.

Project Planning and Design

Agencies and organizations that decide to build a project come to the conclusion to build based on the development of a master plan or capital plan. The master plan is a strategy that addresses the needs for facility improvements and capital investments for rehabilitation and expansion. A master plan generally speaks to a campus or organization that has facilities in a central location or disbursed geographically. The master plan assesses the need for repairs, modernization, upgrades, or new construction and identifies options and solutions to address the needs. It also assesses the availability of federal, state, and local funding and other sources to finance improvements and capital investments and provides an overview of the scope of projects that the Agency may expect to accomplish with existing funds.

The project is born from the master plan. Too many agencies, in an attempt to save money on soft costs, bring in the Construction Manager after important decisions are made. Certainly, the Construction Manager can play a key role at the start of a project, early in the concept phase. The Agency / Owner and the design team are going to make key decisions that will bear down on the construction project. These include defining the scope of the project, planning, financing the project, and transmitting project goals to your team. One of the first things that needs to be done in project planning is to define the scope of the work. This is one of the Agency's most important responsibilities because the scoping of a project can be vexing. The challenge is to identify the need, balance the need with available funding, and figure out the best and most cost effective way to achieve the goal without compromising on quality and the functionality of the facility or end product. The scoping of a project sets the parameters for design, and the Architect will be developing design objectives based on this important step.

If we are going to build something new, there are a number of questions to be asked and answered. For example:

- How many staff will be housed in the facility?
- What is the size and functionality of equipment and systems to be installed?
- What is the expected life of the building?
- Will the building be designed for sustainability or LEED certification?
- What are the considerations for operating costs in the future?

It will cost much less to change the scope of the project in the planning phase than in advanced design, or heaven forbid, during construction. As planning progresses into design, the cost to make changes increases. Once the project is into construction, now we are talking about change orders, schedule changes, changes in material requirements, and other frightful things. Once we have constructed the building, forget about it! It is obviously in the Agency's interest to ensure that the project is properly scoped in the early planning stage. If the project is scoped properly, it will be affordable, it will function as intended, the building systems will be properly sized, and everything will fit.

This is the optimum time to bring in the Construction Manager, as the Owner's Agent, assuming this is the model for the project. The Construction Manager can be made responsible to the Agency for managing the planning process, followed by design, construction, and post construction phases. In planning, the Construction Manager should be tasked with assisting in the optimum use of available funds and controlling the scope of the work. As the project moves to design, the Construction Manager will assist in enhancing the design and this will impact on construction quality.

Once the project is in the design phase, agencies require submission at certain points of completion of the project. Design milestones that frequently require submission of design for review by the Agency include: conceptual design, schematic design, design development, 60 percent of completion, 90 percent of completion, and 100% of completion. The Agency will be reviewing the design to ensure that it meets the expectations of the Owner. This is where any misunderstandings about the scope and direction of the project surface. In fast track design build contracts, work begins before all design is complete, so in these cases drawings and specifications are reviewed as they are completed. Agency reviews do not relieve the Architect/Engineer of responsibilities or the consequences of errors and omissions.

Constructability Review

The Construction Manager plays a key role in the review of the documents that are in development. **Constructability review** is performed in order to determine that the project can be constructed based on the design of the Architect/Engineer, the intent of the construction documents, and within cost and schedule parameters. This is a cooperative effort that involves the Agency / Owner, user of the facility, and the design team. The result is a formal, structured review of the documents, and the identification of issues and pitfalls that may arise without revision of the construction documents. Constructability addresses *buildability* and *bidability*. The scope of review is focused on the following:

- The documents are clear and consistent
- Sequencing of work can be achieved based on the documents
- The project schedule accurately reflects the sequencing of construction activities
- Construction cost estimates are reasonable considering the project scope
- The impact on the facility operation has been considered
- The impact on other construction activities has been considered
- Site logistics have been considered, such as mobilization requirements, storage of materials, field office facilities, construction traffic, etc.
- Temporary facilities have been provided for
- All required permits have been applied for
- Environmental requirements are addressed such as dewatering of the site, hazardous materials abatement, disposition of hazardous materials, etc.
- Review of architectural drawings
- Review of mechanical, electrical and plumbing systems

Following is an example of the constructability review items required to be performed by resident engineers retained by Pennsylvania Department of Transportation (Penn DOT) for its highway design projects. Note how the criterion listed is designed to ensure that all information required for design is identified, and the requirement to review the plans and specifications for consistency.

Penn DOT Constructability List

- Site logistics and constraints,
- Environmental impacts of proposed construction methods,
- Clarity of documents,
- Technical constructability,
- Compatibility of contract plans, specifications, and standards,
- Subsurface soil data,
- Scheduling requirements,
- Construction phasing,

- Erosion and sedimentation control,
- Maintenance and protection of traffic (MPT),
- Construction site access for each phase of MPT, including material delivery and specialized equipment needs,
- Local event conflicts,
- Material acquisition,
- Utility clearances for constructability and project schedule,
- Property/business Owner access and pedestrian safety/access, and
- Full-scale structural analysis of bridge designs will not be completed as part of the scope of work.
- Constructability reviews establish project duration, milestone dates and restrictions.
- CPM schedule is compatible with Penn DOT specifications.

The intent of the constructability review is a check for buildability and bidability. *Buildability* is the check for the completeness of the drawings, including a cross check between the architectural, electrical, mechanical, plumbing, civil, structural, and landscape architectural drawings, to coordinate such items as pipe sizes and locations, power requirements, structural layout, and other major components. Critical dimensions are reviewed to prevent delay in the construction phase.

Bidability is the extensive review of details, notes, sections, site plans, elevations and contract specifications. The intent is to eliminate ambiguity and conflict, omissions, and other mistakes. There should be little left to interpretation, so that pricing is based on the intent. This will also eliminate some of the Requests for Information that contractors will be issuing later on when inconsistencies and ambiguities are identified.

Value Engineering

Value Engineering (VE) (sometimes referred to as Value Management) was pioneered by General Electric Corporation during World War II, when workers and materials were scarce, and is used today in construction to implement a systematic process using a team from a variety of disciplines to analyze the functions of a project to improve the value from investment.

The VE process examines the value of design; construction; maintenance; contractor; state, local and federal approval agencies; other stakeholders; and the public. The VE process is chaired by a facilitator provided by the Agency. The Construction Manager can facilitate the VE sessions or participate as a member of the VE team. The major project components are identified, their functions are determined, and the estimated cost of each component is identified. The intent is to identify project components that will have little impact, if any, on the design intent, and can be reviewed for downsizing, elimination or replacement. Project components that are necessary but are at a high cost are also evaluated to determine means to save cost without compromising quality or functionality.

Bid and Award

From the Construction Manager's point of view, the Agency has provided its full commitment to the project, and has made the funding available. The design is complete, and the Construction Manager has assembled or assisted in the final preparation of the construction contract documents. Contractors are limited in their ability to successfully bid and perform work. First, the bonding capacity needs to be in place. Second, the Contractor's backlog of work will affect the ability to obtain the bond, since bonding is based on the company's stability, backlog of work, management capability and experience. If the company is too close to the upper end of the bonding limit, the surety is not likely to issue the bonds.

The Contractor's bid is based on the total of direct and indirect costs. Direct costs are: materials, equipment, the cost of subcontractors, and job overhead. Indirect costs are the costs of corporate overhead, contingency and profit.

As the day of the bid approaches, the Construction Manager will provide for escorted site visits with prospective bidders, and will conduct a pre-bid meeting so that the bidders can meet with the design team, the Agency and other project stakeholders to ask questions or request clarification on items in the construction contract documents, prior to bidding. The clarifications must be issued to all plan holders as an addendum to the bid package.

When the bids are received and opened, a bid tabulation will be prepared to record all of the bids along with the final cost estimate that has been prepared as a control to compare against the bids. After the bid openings, the Construction Manager will review the bids and determine whether a recommendation for the award of the contract will be made to the low bidder. Before a recommendation to award, the following will be considered:

- Are the bids within the budget?
- How many bids were received? Was there adequate competition in the bidding?
- How close were the bids to the estimate?
- Does the bid amount fairly represent the project scope?
- Is the low bidder qualified to do the project?

The review of the bids will generally include the Owner/Agency, Architect / Engineer and Construction Manager. If a decision is made to proceed with a bid that exceeds the project budget, funding availability must be confirmed. The Construction Manager proceeds with a recommendation for award, and the Agency will issue the Notice of Award, unless the CM is directly holding the contract, in which case the CM may issue this, depending on procedure.

A key element of review of the bids is focused on whether or not the bid is a **balanced bid**. A mathematically unbalanced bid contains lump sum or unit bid items that do not reflect reasonable actual costs and a reasonable proportionate share of the bidder's anticipated profit, overhead and other indirect costs. In effect, it is structured on nominal prices for some work items and inflated prices for other work items. The bid should actually reflect a proportionate share of the total cost of the work plus a fair allocation of profit for that proportion of the work. To determine if the bid is unbalanced, it needs to be evaluated by the Construction Manager for reasonable conformance with the final construction control estimate. The question to be answered is why the bid is unbalanced and what effect the unbalanced bid would have on the contract.

Unbalanced bids occur for various reasons. When a bidder intentionally overprices work done early in the project, it is an attempt to get more money up front, and this is known as *"front loading"* the contract. This also causes the bid to be materially unbalanced, which means that it is tantamount to an advanced payment, which is probably prohibited by law and agency contracting requirements. Contractors also submit unbalanced bids to maximize profits by overpricing bid items that will be used in greater quantities than the Contractor believes was estimated in the bid, and by under pricing items that the Contractor believes will be in substantially lesser quantities.

When it is determined that a bid is balanced, and the contract is awarded, the Construction Manager will work with the Contractor to develop the **Schedule of Values.** This is a detailed statement that outlines the pay items of work that constitute the total bid sum. It is an allocation of values for the various items of work and is also used as the basis for submitting and reviewing progress payments.

In the award phase of the project, the Contractor should be busy with pre-project planning activity. This is the time when the Contractor and the Construction Manager can begin to plan many of the project details. The project schedule is submitted by the Contractor to the Construction Manager in this period. The award period ends when the contract is executed and a Notice to Proceed has been issued by the Agency.

Construction Phase

The basic functions of the Construction Manager during the construction phase of the project include:

- Reporting on progress of the project
- Construction scheduling and monitoring
- Construction cost control
- Shop drawings and submittal monitoring
- Construction supervision
- Completion
- Start-Up

Progress Reports

Progress reports inform the Agency about the status of the project. It is submitted at regular intervals, such as monthly, throughout the life of the project. It lets the stakeholders know whether work is progressing satisfactorily, that is within the project's budget and approved schedule.

The Progress Report submitted by the Construction Manager should have an executive summary, description of work completed, work scheduled, project issues, proposed resolutions, progress of the schedule and project cost information.

The Executive Summary provide a summary that includes a description of the project progress to date, milestone dates achieved, status of costs compared to budget, change order information, and other pertinent information highlighted from the report.

The body of the report should describe the progress of the work in the reporting period, with emphasis on major work elements completed or in progress in the period. Information should also be provided for Requests for Information (RFI) status, approved change orders with cost and time, pending change orders, work activities planned for the next period or month, progress photos, the open submittal log, and project cost summaries including costs to date compared to the project budget.

Construction Scheduling and Monitoring

The Construction Manager will use the schedule as a management tool to confirm that the original plan is being carried out, and by obtaining the commitment of those parties who must perform to carry out their part of the plan. The schedule will also be used to aid in determining and implementing appropriate action when there are performance deviations. The Construction Manager will be directing the development of the baseline schedule and ensure that it is updated as the project progresses.

The Construction Manager is obligated to provide you with superior knowledge of your project, and the ability for you to track the direction of the project.

The Construction Manager will be expected to ensure that there is a comprehensive scheduling effort, with attention to construction details and component relationships, so that proper sequencing occurs and the project remains on track with the calendar. Remember that your contract requires construction contractors and their subcontractors to provide timely compliance of their work, provide adequate labor, and perform the work so that it does not interfere with other operations that would screw up the orderly sequencing of work. It is important that the Agency's contract with the Contractor specify that time is of the essence, and that the Contractor is bound to do what is necessary to meet the schedule.

When required, the Construction Manager will be meeting to discuss realistic activity sequences and durations, the allocation of labor and materials, the prompt submittal and processing of shop drawings and samples, and monitoring the delivery of products that require long lead time procurement. The Construction Manager will use the scheduling tool to identify potential variances between the schedule and actual work, and to recommend adjustments and revisions to correct or pre-empt schedule delays.

Project Engineering

The office functions involved in the administration of the project are referred to generally as **project engineering**. This may be provided by staff classified as Project Engineers, Office Engineers, or may be a shared responsibility between the Project Manager and designated staff, depending on the size and staffing of the project. Through the project engineering function, the Construction Manager will:

- Prepare complete, accurate and timely submittal logs for construction projects based on project drawings and specifications
- Be accountable for receiving approved submittals from Architect or Engineer and notifying the Project Superintendent of potential schedule impact
- Prepare necessary back-up for change requests
- Complete all required project close-out documents per contract
- Distribute contract documents to subcontractors, including drawings, specifications, and general conditions. Include any accepted alternates or addendums with documents
- Distribute final requirement documentation to subcontractors and bookkeeper
- Schedule all required construction meetings with required personnel, subcontractors, architects and owners
- Take accurate and complete meeting minutes and distribute timely
- Organize, prepare agendas for, and write minutes for Owner/Architect pre-bid, project and closeout meetings
- Solicit subcontractors and suppliers for proposal prior to proposal submission time
- Prepare contracts and change orders for execution
- Submit request for surety bond(s) and insurance certificates. Submit with signed contract to Owner
- Prepare correspondence with the Agency, architect, engineers, subcontractors, suppliers, etc. Examples of referenced correspondence include, but not confined to the following items: Schedule of Values, project schedule,

memos, and requests for information, transmittals and submittals
- Submit building permit application, follow-up on review progress and receive upon approval. Submit Check Request to Finance for associated fees according to Check Request procedures
- During Construction Phase, proactively manage project to achieve quality, schedule, budget and safety. Utilize and maintain tools: schedule and document management to track and record project performance
- Maintain project level relations and conduct project meetings. Ensure prompt payment processing according to percentage complete timely upon receipt from Owner
- Document quality and progress of each Subcontractor and Suppliers. Update Subcontractors and Suppliers of any changes to the plans, specifications and/or schedule
- Inform the Agency through the Project Manager of productivity, costs, quality control, document management and processing of applications for payment. Notify the Project Manager of any issues that may arise, affecting quality, budget, progress and safety
- Monitor staffing needs, evaluate performance, and address employee relation issues as warranted for staff

Issues of Productivity

We have stated before that on the project, time is of the essence. Many things can happen to conspire against meeting a schedule. The Construction Manager needs to have the experience and expertise to identify and dispatch those practices and issues that may arise, nipping them in the bud before they loom over the project. Obviously, not everything is in the control of the Construction Manager, and when issues may arise that could hamper productivity, the Construction Manager needs to act decisively, and the it is in the Agency's best interest to allow the Construction Manager to make field decisions. When a project is planned and a schedule is drawn up, there are basic assumptions and expectations that give credence to the schedule.

First and foremost are expectations that:

- Labor at the site will be productive
- There will be access to the site when required

- Materials will arrive when needed
- Logistics are worked out for lay-down and mobilization
- Project design is constructable
- Unusual conditions have been identified and planned for
- Management capacity exists to run the job properly at all levels

Well, as the great poet Robert Burns once wrote, "the best laid plans of mice and men often go astray". Even the best thought out plans can go wrong. For example, there may be physical limitations on the project site that simply do not allow you to throw manpower into the project to expedite the work. In this case, the doubling of input (more labor) will not result in the doubling of output (construction). Congestion of this type can be the result of changed site conditions, changes in sequence, changes in design, or simply the rush to complete a job by a milestone deadline. Congestion among the trades as described here is sometimes referred to as *"stacking the trades"*.

When the Construction Manager is monitoring the work, or reviewing a change order, a basic assumption will be whether the Contractor's workforce can perform its work with minimal interference from other trades. Many times the Contractor does not plan for the impact of stacking of trades will have on labor production. The Construction Manager, in these cases must be able to work with the Contractor to figure out the options that are available to avoid a decrease in production. This may involve such strategies as changing the work sequence, changing crew composition, changing work hours, or revising construction methods. Any or all of these strategies have proven effective in improving productivity in these circumstances. The Construction Manager must have the experience to understand the causes of stacking of trades, and employing methods to maintain expected productivity levels.

Other factors can also work against productivity. Much has to do with "attitude" and morale at the site. Again, the Construction Manager helps to set the tone for the relations on the project site.

Poor cooperation between trades, excessive criticism, poor supervision, excessive or abrupt changes, inefficient management of materials, and other factors lead to a non-positive environment that affects productivity. Here, the leadership exercised by the Construction Manager and the Agency are critical to maintaining a positive environment at the site. In short, the Construction Manager must always be aware of the current levels of productivity and ways to improve production to meet deadlines.

Project Superintendence

Project superintendence is the planning, administration and supervision of the actual construction in the field. The personnel provided by the Construction Manager for this function must be competent constructors who can maintain professionalism on the site that maintains respect for all contractors and subcontractors at the site, while exercising authority and discipline to get the work accomplished.

Staffing for Superindence

The personnel hired by the Construction Manager and the Contractors on your project site must have knowledge of all phases of building construction, including work performed by various building trades. This includes knowledge of mechanical, electrical, mechanical and structural systems, building materials, tools, machines, construction safety, the ability to read and apply the plans and specifications and other construction contract documents to determine compliance. Project superindents also need to have supervisory ability, interpersonal skills and ability to communicate verbally and in writing.

Staffing the project by the Construction Manager to perform the functions of project superintendence depends on several factors: the size, scope and complexity of the project, and the amount of funding the Agency is willing to provide for these services. On a very large project, superintendence personnel may include: the Project Manager, a General Superintendent, a mechanical, electrical and plumbing (MEP) coordinator (also referred at times to as MEP Project Manager, Superintendent or inspector). On smaller projects, the entire team may consist of a Project Manager and a Superintendent or inspector, aided by an office engineer, or even less staff than this. In any case, when the CM accepts the funding level for services and signs the contract, the Agency should expect and demand full services in accordance with the scope of the contract.

The **Project Manager** executes the work plans for field superintendence and identifies the reasons needed and assigns individual responsibilities for the supervision and coordination of the work. The Project Manager has the ultimate responsibility for managing day to day operational aspects of the project, reviews deliverables, and implements the quality assurance program for compliance with design intent and the construction contract documents.

The **General Superintendent** is a supervisory Superintendent, to whom construction Superintendents and inspectors report to. This position coordinates and supervises the activities of the Construction Manager's Superintendents who are deployed in the field to monitor and supervise particular aspects or locations of work. The General Superintendent is responsible for the entire project, ensuring that construction work is progressing according to schedule, and to ensure that necessary manpower, equipment and material is on site. This position plans oversees planning and the use of project resources, and provides for necessary coordination with the Agency and facility users on site. He or she is responsible to ensure that the administration of jobs is effective and efficient, that the field forces are well organized, and troubleshoots difficult construction problems. The General Superintendent also finds ways to motivate and keep personnel / subcontractors / suppliers and service providers' morale at a high level, establishes action plans and their implementation in order to achieve goals, oversees job schedules and ensures that they are updated and reported, and strives to keep the Agency satisfied.

The **MEP Superintendent** or inspector is responsible for managing all components of a construction project related to the mechanical, electrical and plumbing, or MEP, elements of the facility. This position not only requires technical knowledge of the various building systems, but also management skills necessary to coordinate the work of various trades and sequencing of work so that trades are not stacked.

Project Superintendents and **Construction Inspectors**, on large projects, report to the General Superintendent. Where the role of General Superintendent is assumed by the Project Manager, then they report directly to him. These personnel may be assigned to a particular aspect of work or geographic location within the project site. They inspect construction progress to ensure that procedures and materials comply with specifications; observe work in progress to assure conformance with requirements and acceptable workmanship. They review contract plans and specifications for compliance with appropriate building codes and project requirements, prepare daily inspection reports, and ensure that the

Contractor is following its approved safety plan. In some cases, the project may be large enough to employ a full time safety engineer or inspector, or to perform safety inspections and audits on an interim basis. We will discuss safety in more detail in another chapter.

Site superintendence functions include the following:

- Ensure that there is adequate manpower in the field with the required equipment and supplies necessary to carry out scheduled work
- Ensure coordination of the trades, so that there is no interference between one work component and another
- Work with the Project Manager and Project Engineer to develop, review and revise the progress schedule, using the schedule as a management tool to improve performance
- Identify field construction and work sequence issues so that these may be addressed
- Monitoring actual work performed by all parties, and working to bring deviations from plan back in line
- Preparing daily reports and other required documentation to be used to support or defend against claims, requests for change, and approval of payment requisitions
- Assure implementation of quality assurance including inspection for compliance for work that is placed and required testing for materials and systems

Management of the Project Site

The CM must take full control of the project site. This will involve everything required for the management, construction inspection, security, safety, material staging and handling, site access, and the management of personnel involved in the project. If your site is within or adjacent to occupied facilities, the Construction Manager is responsible for erecting a wall of construction, meaning a separation of activity and manpower within the project confines, to the rest of the site.

The project site logistics planning by the Construction Manager in the early stages of a project will result in the avoidance of many problems as the pace of construction quickens. The Construction

Manager's site logistics plan should provide for:

- Maintenance of a secure site
- Entry and egress control
- Designated parking areas (if available on the site)
- Paths of travel for construction traffic
- Strategic placement of the field office for easy access and proximity to utilities and in an area that affords maximum visibility to the area under construction
- Storage areas for material and equipment
- Contractor field office and storage trailers
- Lay-down areas for substantial material placement
- Stakeout for future site utilities to minimize relocations of trailers and materials

The organization, neatness and maintenance of the field office reflects on the professionalism of the Construction Manager. Signage should be easily read to direct vendors, visitors, and deliveries to the proper location on the site. There must also be adequate control of the flow of workers and visitors.

Developing and maintaining good relationships with contractors and subcontractors on the project site is an important function of the Construction Manager, and the Agency should support these efforts, certainly as long as there is good faith on the part of contractors to perform.

The Agency should expect the Construction Manager's Project Manager not to be a "desk jockey". He or she needs to devote some time to the field, monitoring the activities of the Contractor and the Construction Manager's field personnel.

A Project Manager who is deskbound and directing a project without first hand knowledge through observation of site conditions, progress, and field issues, and without being visible and conveying leadership, will not serve the project well. The Construction Manager needs to walk the site and know what is happening on every square foot of the project site.

Coordinating Work Sequences

A very important task is coordinating work sequences of contractors and trade work. Everything needs to fit in the place it is supposed to fit, as specified and designed. It is helpful if the construction contract documents require the Contractor to provide coordination drawings, such as for the installation of MEP systems above a ceiling. In this way, all contractors and trades involved in the installation of work that needs to be coordinated, such as the construction of the aforementioned ceiling will help to determine that everything will be installed as designed. It may come to pass that there needs to be modifications. To continue with the example of the ceiling, perhaps modifications to fixtures, ductwork, the reflective ceiling plan for lighting, and other changes might be necessary for proper installation and construction. The Construction Manager, in cases like this, will want to bring the Architect in to review the coordination drawings. Now, let's assume that there is no requirement for coordination drawings. In this case, you still need to have a Construction Manager that is proactive, meeting with the Contractor and subcontractors to resolve coordination issues. Where the design is deficient and there is out of scope work, the Construction Manager will need to assess any requests for change orders by the Contractor.

Schedule Management

Schedule management is a critical function of the Construction Manager. At the beginning of the project, the Construction Manager has met with the Contractors at the project site and has reviewed the construction schedule and required work activities and sequences. The Contractors should have been required to review this baseline schedule, and determine with the Construction Manager whether there are changes that should be made for valid reasons. The Contractor may be required to provide a "Two Week Look Ahead Schedule". The review of the *look ahead schedule* (which can be one week, three weeks, or whatever the process requires) is to determine whether the project is on track to meet or beat productivity and cost for the snapshot period projected by the look ahead schedule. Related to this review, is the review of the status of all submittals and timely responses, arrival of material and equipment, and sufficient labor required for current and near term activities.

Typically, the Construction Manager will be monitoring the project schedule based on milestones. A milestone is a significant event centered on the completion of a major project deliverable. There are several types of milestones on the project. Milestones have ramifications to the schedule, because they are benchmarks for start up times, progress expectations, and completion deadlines. For example, work cannot start until all permits are in place. A milestone date is established for this. Work must be completed in a certain time frame due to requirements or constraints. This is another milestone date. The project must be completed by the end of a certain period because it must be occupied on an established date. This is the milestone date for completion.

There are times when extensions of time are legitimate. In these cases, the Construction Manager needs to be as fair and objective as possible and advise the Agency of the need to provide extensions of time and to modify the schedule accordingly. Sometimes, although there may be recognition that there have been delays to the project which would normally result in an extension of time by the Agency, the decision is made to maintain the original project schedule.

When this happens and the Construction Manager is notified to maintain the schedule, the result is a "demand for acceleration". This may be the result of a delay caused by the Agency for some reason, called "Constructive Acceleration" and when the Owner / Agency directs the Contractor to complete the project ahead of schedule, also known as "Actual Acceleration".

Non-Compliance

Quality control and quality assurance is a critical task of the Construction Manager. Project Superintendents are in the field providing daily inspection of work to assure quality and contract compliance. The Architect is also present periodically on site during construction to review conformity with design. Daily inspection reports used by the Construction Manager's personnel must fully document acceptable work quantities that are installed and can be paid. When a contractor fails to meet performance requirements, and verbal communication has failed to correct deficiencies, the non compliance must be documented and communicated to the Contractor with corrective action requirements.

Disputed Work or Requests for Information

Disagreements often arise over issues of the contract scope of work, and differing interpretations of what the contract requires. Scope issues often relate to interpreting the plans and specifications. When this happens, the Contractor will be directed by the Construction Manager to issue a request for clarification. A Request for Information (RFI) is issued to request information, clarification, interpretation, related to plans, specifications and contract requirements. RFIs are also used to request minor changes that do not involve cost or time adjustments and to obtain instructions when there are conflicting contract requirements.

Disputes arise out of delays in getting the work installed, unsatisfactory work or failure to make payments. Most construction contracts address dispute resolution. The intent is to try to resolve disputes without resorting to litigation, arbitration or mediation. Sometimes disputes reach the point of claims under a mechanic's lien. This is when contractors or others involved in the project ensure they are paid for services performed and materials supplied by attaching the property when the work is performed or materials are delivered. In remains on the property until the matter is resolved, such as through payment. It is noted here that there is federal legislation known as *The Miller Act*. This does not permit liens to be placed against federal government property. States have passed similar laws, often referred to as "little Miller Act" also preventing the filing of liens against state and local government property. The claimant must resort to the claims and disputes procedures in the contract.

Many construction contracts require that disputes arising under the contract be resolved by arbitration. This step is usually required before courts will review the case. The dispute is heard by a neutral arbitrator, who hears the case and makes a final decision based on evidence. The courts will not overturn the order of an arbitrator in binding arbitration unless the arbitrator made a decision that is at odds with the law and legal foundations relating to the issues arbitrated.

Mediation is another method of dispute resolution that may be required before a matter can be brought to court. Mediation is used to try to reach mutual agreement for settlement.

Partnering

Many agencies have tried to establish an environment at the outset of the project to come to agreements on how to deal with disputes and to resolve them before they go to formal resolution through arbitration, mediation or litigation. This has been accomplished through partnering. This is a process where the Owner /Agency, Construction Manager, Architect / Engineer, and contractors commit to improve communications and avoid disputes by working together towards shared and common goals and objectives on a project specific basis. If executed properly, partnering can build trust, improve communication, help to eliminate surprises, and avoid adversarial encounters by anticipating and resolving problems through the informal management of conflicts.

Partnering sessions provide for an overview of the project, the project organization, protocols, and lines of communication and how communication flows between the team.

The goals of the project are stated, and key expectations and the needs of each group or stakeholder are discussed. These sessions may identify potential project issues or challenges and strategies and action plans to address these. An issue resolution process I discussed, along with mechanisms for follow-up. A partnering charter is usually developed.

Partnering is not intended to change or relax any terms of the contract, or to circumvent procedures, protocols and processes. Contractors are not expected to give up anything they are entitled to, or to expect extra work without compensation. Partnering is not a panacea, but a professional approach to work toward the common goal of a successful project through increased profitability by contractors, reduction in completion time, reduction in schedule changes, increased safety, reduction of claims and change orders.

Change Orders

The Construction Manager is responsible for managing the change order process during construction. **Change orders** are sometimes the result of requests for changes in scope by the Owner / Agency, requests from the Contractor for non-owner generated changes, and requests for changes based on the belief that the plans and specifications contain omissions or errors.

If the Agency initiates the change order, the Construction Manager should coordinate with the Architect / Engineer and provide drawing and / or specification revisions, sketches, or written descriptions of the changes required. There must be a clear communication of what is being requested, and these changes should be reviewed with the Contractor. If the work involves deletions or additions to the scope, there must be a clear understanding of how extras and credits will be presented.

When the change order is initiated by the Contractor, it must be presented in such a way that the Agency can reasonably evaluate the change and the request for additional funding. This must include a breakdown of labor costs by classification, the number of hours for each classification, plus the burden rate on labor. The cost of materials and equipment must also be documented.

The Construction Manager's input is invaluable in reviewing the proposal and commenting on the reasonableness of cost, including preparing an independent cost estimate for comparison purposes, and determining the impact of the change on the schedule.

Contractor Claims

Claims for additional costs and time extensions happen for many reasons. Contractors who decide to submit a claim must provide a breakdown of additional costs and time, and provide sufficient documentation to back up the claim. The Agency may be relying on its Construction Manager for claims management.

As scheduling techniques become more sophisticated and comprehensive, it has become easier to identify where delays are occurring and how a delay in one activity impacts on other activities. The flip side of our sophistication and the ever greater complexity of our projects is that they increase conditions that yield a higher probability of disputes, conflicting interpretations, and adversarial positions. Significant additional costs can be experienced by the Agency, the Owner or both parties due to the actions of the other parties or parties involved in the project. Claims and disputes arise from deficiencies in the specifications, drawings, restricted access to the site, Owner caused disruptions or delays, disagreements over the definition of substantial completion, interpretations of the construction documents, enforcement of liquidated damages and other matters.

When a claim is received, the questions that need to be answered are:

- Does the Agency or its consultant have any responsibility?
- Was the situation predictable when the contract was executed?
- Were the deficiencies in the construction contract documents?

- Has the contract been misinterpreted?

The Construction Manager needs to communicate with any contractor that is contemplating submittal of a claim. Perhaps the Contractor will not pursue the claim if it can be shown that the grounds for the claim are not strong, or that it is beneficial for the Contractor to maintain good relations by handling the matter in another way that does not compromise the project or the Agency. Despite these efforts by the Construction Manager, the Contractor may believe so strongly that he has an entitlement to time or compensation that the claim is prepared and submitted. The claim must be submitted in writing directly after the cause of the claim. Time is of the essence and the timeline is most likely specified in the contract. The notification to the Agency must make clear references to those contract clauses where compensation or time is being claimed. The rights of the Contractor are in jeopardy if timely notification does not occur. If the claim involves time, the Contractor is requesting a change to contract delivery dates through an adjustment of project milestones in the master schedule due to delays not caused by the Contractor. If the claim involves compensation, this is reimbursement for direct and premium time, increased equipment costs, increased financing cost, increases in site overhead and office overhead, and a decrease in labor productivity. The basis for this is that productivity drops causing an increase in duration required to finish the work, and increases costs to the Contractor.

CPM scheduling techniques are often used by all parties to prepare for or defend against claims. CPM scheduling analysis aids in red flagging delay and the impact on the schedule. Claims may be based on direct cause and effect: if it did not happen, it would not have resulted in delays and increases in cost. Claims may also be more complicated where the request for compensation is based on the claim of an indirect cost or delay due to actions of the Agency / Owner or its agents. This so called "ripple effect" is not easily accepted by agencies because it is not clearly identifiable. The difficulty in settling claims is where there is disagreement on the causes of the loss of productivity.

The Construction Manager as the Agency's agent should be vigilant to possible claims that arise from its actions and the action of the Agency / Owner and its agents. These usually result from work site congestion, the stacking of trades, diversion of resources, poor supervision, restricted access to the site or work areas, and other factors, and to take proactive steps to alert the Agency of these issues in an attempt to avoid potential claims.

In summary, misunderstandings or changes leading to claims and disputes are triggered by:

- Deficiencies in plans and specifications
- Incomplete or inaccurate responses to RFIs and questions
- Inadequate administration and supervision
- Site or building conditions that differ substantially from those depicted in the contract documents
- Extra work or change order work resulting from requests or actions of the Owner/Agency such as disruptions, delays, or acceleration requirements that deviate from the approved baseline schedule
- Breaches of the contract
- Refusal or inability to meet performance or quality standards, resulting form disagreement of contract or design intent

Here are some key points to consider as we close out this discussion about contractor claims:

1. When the Architect specifies a component of work in the design and contract documents, the contractor who follows the design is not responsible for design errors. Courts have held that contractors are not responsible for design errors when the specifications are not suitable for the intended result, and not because of faulty materials or poor workmanship. Even if there are contract clauses requiring the general contractor to notify the Architect of changes needed to ensure compliance, the contractor has, in effect, a guarantee that the design is buildable in most cases. Many disputes arise because of unknown site conditions, such as subsurface or changed conditions. The contractor cannot be expected to have sufficient knowledge of site conditions not disclosed by the construction documents. It is unfair to expect that a contractor cannot rely on geotechnical or other engineering

reports provided by the Agency. The contractor must be able to show that the contract documents were inaccurate or misleading, or that the bid was based on misleading documents provided by the Agency. This does not mean, however, that the contractor is submitting a legitimate claim for any obvious conditions that could have been observed during a prebid site visit. Here the Construction Manager can assist the Agency in determining if the physical conditions triggering the claim were unknown, whether actual conditions reflect the contract documents and the bid received from the contractor, cost claims are based solely on the materially different conditions encountered, and that costs and delays actually occurred because of the encountered conditions.

2. Claims are sometimes based on the contention of errors and omissions by the Architect/Engineer. On a large and complex project, it may be reasonable to encounter some minor lack of detail, coordination, or dimensions. Most problems arise from certain factors: (a). Poor coordination with MEP, structural and architectural trades; (b). Conflicts within the construction contract documents; (c). Boilerplate requirements that were cut and pasted from other contracts that do not apply to this one; (d). Lack of communication between the design consultants at the time of the design; (e) Insufficient consultation with the Owner /agency at the time of design resulting in required changes in construction; and (f). Insufficient time devoted to design and constructability review before incorporation of these documents into the bidding documents.

3. Claims resulting from acceleration are based on excusable delays that entitle the contractor to an extension in time. For some reason, the Agency may deny a request for more time and require the acceleration of work, maintaining the current schedule. In a case like this, it is likely that the

contractor will document all costs associated with acceleration and will notify the Construction Manager of an intent to file a claim if a change order for a time extension and money for additional costs is denied.

4. The contract documents used by the Agency will specify the process for the submission of a claim. The contract should require that the contractor must continue work while a claim is pending, and that the contractor will be declared delinquent in its work if it does not continue to perform. It should be the Agency's and the Construction Manager's position that a properly documented claim will be reviewed and that an attempt at resolution by mutual agreement will be made. If the claim cannot be resolved at this level, a decision will be made by the Agency and submitted within a specified time frame to the contractor, who acknowledges receipt of the decision and whether the decision is accepted or rejected. If the claim is rejected, the Contractor's remedy will be arbitration, mediation or litigation.

5. The Agency's Construction Manager must be able to work with the Agency, its attorneys, and other consultants and prepare an administrative file that includes all correspondences, daily reports, inspection reports, test reports, payment requests, job progress schedules, time and payroll records, job progress photos, estimates, bids and quotations, change order proposals, requests and estimates, and any as-built drawings that are interim or completed.

Project Closeout

The last phase of the project is the **Project Closeout**. The purpose of the project closeout is to obtain conditional occupancy and final acceptance of the project deliverables. The Agency has determined at this point that the project has met the goals established and the contractor has complied with the contract documents. This is the point where the project is substantially complete. The project is substantially complete where the Agency could actually occupy or utilize the project facility for the purposes intended.

When the Contractor considers the project to have reached this level, the Contractor should notify the Construction Manager to request an inspection. Substantial completion must be agreed to by all parties. Satisfaction that the "punch list" of the remaining work can be accomplished in a reasonable timeframe should be reviewed before committing to substantial completion. If there are extensive punch list items (items that need to be completed by the contractor to achieve full contract compliance), then we are not at the point of substantial completion. The Agency should not assume responsibility for the facility until substantial completion occurs, or else it assumes responsibility for such items as maintenance, security, utilities, damage, and insurance once the project is accepted as substantially complete. Normally substantial completion is approved before there is a request for final payment. A certificate of final completion signifies that the project, and all punch list items, are 100% complete. The contractor will submit a request for final payment shortly after the Certificate of Final Completion has been executed.

The Construction Manager should secure a release of liens and claims, completed by the contractor and submitted with final payment requests. The contractor, by executing this document, is certifying that they have been paid and have satisfied all contractual obligations. This process also assures the Agency that proper payments have been made to subcontractors and suppliers with public agency funds that have been paid to the contractor.

Consent of surety is a document submitted by the contractor. The surety agrees that the final payment oft the contractor does not relieve the surety of any of its obligations under the bond issued for the project.

Prior to occupancy the Agency must verify the safety of the interior and exterior of the facility. This is a critical stage of the project because the Agency assumes responsibility for allowing occupants to work or visit the building. All systems, equipment, and areas must be inspected to ensure their proper and safe operation. This review and verification should take place prior to approving substantial completion. Finally, the Agency must receive from its Architect / Engineer and / or Construction Manager, the following documents, before final payment is made:

- Certification of Punch List Completion

- Required manufacturers warranties

- Maintenance & Operational Manuals
- Final Plumbing Inspections
- As Built and Shop Drawings for Inclusion by Design Professional in the Record Drawings, CD-Rom (one for agency and one for ABA)
- Contractor's One-Year Warranty
- Certificate of Air Balance
- Final HVAC Inspection

Chapter 8 References
The following sources were utilized in writing this chapter:

Capstone: The History of CM Practice and Procedures. Construction Management Association of America. 2010.

Construction Management Standards of Practice. Construction Management Association of America. 2010.

Civitello, A. Construction Operations Manual of Policies and Procedures Third Ed 2000. McGraw-Hill Companies, New York, NY

Hanna, A., Russell, J, and Emerson, E. "Report – Stacking the Trades for Electrical Contractors. http://www.electri.org/ekn/ekn.aspx?id=299

Levy, S. Construction Superintendent's Operations Manual. 2004. McGraw-Hill Companies, New York, NY

Schexnayder, C., and Mayo, R. Construction Management Fundamentals. McGraw-Hill 1st Edition. 2004

U.S. Army Corps of Engineering, New York District. "Value Engineering". http://www.nan.usace.army.mil/business/buslinks/valueeng/

CHAPTER 9
QUALITY ASSURANCE

WHAT IS QUALITY?

In construction, **quality** means that the stated requirements have been met or exceeded. Quality is not subjective, nor is it intangible. In fact it is very measurable. Every activity on your project must have an accurate description of the completed item and time of performance. This allows for a mechanism to measure compliance and performance. The contract specifications must specify the specific processes and materials to be used. These are the parameters for quality. Quality does not only apply to materials and workmanship on your project. Let's add to this: finishing on time, within budget, without claims and lawsuits, and safely constructed.

ISO 9000

There is a movement that emphasizes quality in all industries, not only construction. International Quality Standards have been defined by ISO 9000. ISO is the International Organization for Standardization. ISO 9000 contains quality standards. Quality management systems of ISO certified firms ensure that there are processes and systems in place to achieve quality. ISO is important because it provides internationally accepted systems and the organizational commitment of resources, technology, policies, record keeping and procedures required for managing a quality system.

Quality Assurance and Quality Control

Quality Assurance (QA) refers to the management systems used by construction and design firms to produce high quality work on a consistent basis. This is accomplished by hiring qualified personnel, providing for training, incentives and rewards for high quality performance, procurement systems to hire the best qualified subcontractors and vendors, and personnel policies in place to reduce turnover and retain qualified staff.

Quality Control (QC) refers to the inspection of work to ensure that it meets quality standards required by the construction contract. For example, construction inspectors assigned to highway construction projects are performing a QC function by inspecting the work for compliance with the construction contract documents. They not only inspect work being installed but perform or monitor testing for quality, such as density of soils, slump and compressive strength of concrete, and the temperature of asphalt that arrives on site.

Total quality management (TQM) is a quality management concept pioneered by professor W. Edwards Deming, who was instrumental in applying TQM to manufacturing processes in Japan, leading to Japan's reputation for producing quality products. As applied to construction, it is intended for reducing errors in design and construction methodology, increase client satisfaction, and provide a high level of training to employees, so that they perform at their maximum potential.

Another business management strategy aimed at Quality is called **Six Sigma**. This was originally developed by Motorola. Its premise is to identify factors that contribute to deficiencies and to remove them, resulting in more consistency in process. It includes quality management standards, including the use of designated personnel (known as "Black Belts", "Green Belts", etc.) who have expertise in these methods.

Quality through Inspection

One of the most labor intensive functions of your consultants in the field, whether they are Construction Manager or the Architect /Engineer, (or both) is to provide superintendence and

construction inspections. In order to provide a comprehensive inspection process as part of the Quality Control program for your project, there must be a thorough understanding by Superintendents and inspectors working as the agent of the Agency through the Construction Manager, of all construction contract documents, applicable building codes, and standard industry practices.

Planning for Inspection

The first step in preparing for a construction inspection program is to organize a complete system of construction records. These will include:

- A daily log book and daily report system
- Progress reports on a periodic basis
- Correspondence file
- Change order file
- Payment file
- Shop drawing and sample submittal file
- Substitution file
- Test and inspection file
- Site conference and meeting minutes
- Job memo files
- A complete set of contract documents
- Access to all applicable codes and standards for the work
- Agency requirements where they have jurisdiction over the project such as the Department of Building, the Fire Department, Department of Environmental Protection, etc.
- Schedule of values for pay items that are placed in accordance with the contract and are acceptable
- Contractor safety plan
- Two week look ahead schedule from the contractor
- Access to manufacturer's literature and instructions

Implementing the Inspection Program

The inspector or construction Superintendent will be following inspection criteria for the work that is being installed. The inspector, on a day to day basis will:

- Inspect work to determine compliance with the plans, specifications and other applicable requirements
- Observe actual progress in comparison with the schedule
- Record and report conditions that delay progress
- Keep an accurate record of time and materials, and force account work
- Obtain concurrence from contractor in writing on a daily basis for labor, materials and equipment being used
- Observe delivery of materials and equipment.
- Record and report damages or non-compliance issues

It is important for inspectors not to authorize any deviations from the contract documents, nor to interfere with the work of the contractor or assume responsibility for performance of the contractor's work. The inspector needs to follow a chain of command, and the Agency or Owner should not direct the inspector, but follow protocols for communication to the Project Manager for construction management and the Architect/Engineer.

The inspector is not managing the contractor safety program, and cannot assume responsibility for safety procedures. This does not however relieve the inspector or Superintendent from reporting safety hazards, especially if there is an imminent threat to life, health or safety.

Inspector's Daily Report

Inspectors and construction Superintendents must complete an inspector's **daily report.** Information entered includes the date, the weather, site conditions, contract time status, work forces on the job by trade, equipment on site, material deliveries, visitors to the site, and other pertinent information. In addition, a field memorandum format, consecutively numbered, should be used to elaborate on project issues in the daily report, as required.

Inspections – Starting Up

Daily inspection of work is performed to monitor and document compliance with the construction contract documents, identify deficiencies, document them, and flag items that require corrective action.

At the start of the project, Superintendent and inspection personnel will obtain a project directory of all project stakeholders that may need to be consulted during field operations, including all parties, firms, client, Architect/Engineer, contractors, subcontractors, vendors, suppliers, etc. Emergency phone numbers and other contact information is also obtained. Work cannot start without all permits and agency approvals in place. Before work is started, a check on the progress of record drawings is necessary to make sure that all required documents have been submitted. A schedule of values for pay items must also be obtained, as the inspector or Superintendent will refer to this when signing off on quantities that are acceptable for payment. There are constraints and restrictions that are contained in supplemental or general conditions of the contract, that must be adhered to, such as the limits of construction, paths of travel, safety program, tree and plant protection, special noise and dust control requirements, sediment control and other conditions of the contract.

General Inspection

- Standard inspection procedures will be followed for the receipt and storage of materials delivered to the site. Materials and equipment will be inspected for damage in transit. Materials will be identified by tags or other types of marking, to include type, size, material, gauge, weight, grade, treatment, color, finish, etc. These must meet the contract specifications
- Required certificates, affidavits, and other documents required from the vendor or supplier must be collected. Once materials arrive, they must be properly stored and protected. Materials should not be delivered for out of sequence work unless there are provisions for storage and protection

- Adequate equipment, tools and manpower must be available at the site for the planned for activities
- Installation is coordinated with other trades to avoid interference and stacking of trades
- Approved shop drawings and samples are on site before installation
- Existing and adjacent work connections and tie-in are performed as required
- Laboratory tests, reports and off-site inspections have been performed and documented
- Temperature and climatic conditions are suitable for installation
- Adjacent areas are adequately protected from damage during operations
- Installed work is properly protected
- Inspections are timely, so that deficiencies in material or workmanship are identified promptly
- The Architect / Engineer is provided timely notification for inspection before work they need to review is closed up
- Agency inspections have been performed as required before work is closed up
- Cleaning and maintenance is performed as required at the site
- Safety programs are in place and being implemented by the contractor
- The site is properly secured by fencing, locks, and security, as applicable
- Nothing is left unattended at the end of the day, and everything is secured

Construction Inspection of Technical Items

All work items in each division of the contract require inspection by the Superintendent or construction inspector in real time as work is being installed. The technical areas of inspection include:

- General Requirements of the contract
- Site Work including earthwork, landscaping, foundations, utilities

- Concrete operations
- Structural steel, metal joists and decking
- Exterior work including roofing, thermal protection, structures, doors and windows, curtainwall
- Thermal and moisture protection including insulation, waterproofing
- Wood, including rough carpentry, prefabricated structural wood, finish carpentry and architectural woodwork
- Finishes including lath and plaster, drywall, tile, terrazzo, wood flooring, painting
- Mechanical systems including HVAC, plumbing, fire protection, heat generation and refrigeration
- Electrical systems including service and distribution, lighting, fire alarms, and communications
- Specialties, equipment, furnishings, special construction and conveying systems

Contractor's Responsibility for Quality

The contractor is obligated to establish and maintain a quality program under the provisions of the contract with the Agency. The contractor's quality plan should include the following:

- Contractor management plan for quality
- Procedures for Quality Control inspection by the contractor
- Contractor document control
- Subcontractor pre-qualification and evaluation procedures
- Handling, storage, and control of equipment at the site
- Inspection and testing procedures
- Field acceptance process
- Calibration of equipment used in construction
- Non-conformance procedures for remedial action
- Submittal logs
- Maintenance of quality records
- Certification and training programs
- Designation of a Quality Control Program representative

Internal meetings at the outset of a project should include a review of the responsibilities of the Project Manager and construction Superintendents. A review of the contract documents in detail and the scope of work should be performed for familiarity and to identify any potential shortcomings or problems. This is a good time to develop a relationship with the Architect and the Construction Manager to discuss these issues, and to establish a professional relationship with the Agency's representatives. This meeting should also include the following agenda items:

- Safety program and OSHA compliance
- Pre-installation meetings required for new operations in the field
- Methodology for internal inspections of work and testing procedures
- Required mock-ups
- Controlling the quality of subcontractor work
- Responsibility for the shop drawings submittal log and review of status of submittals
- Status of buyouts
- Site logistics and availability for proper storage of materials and equipment
- Preparation of as-builts by the contractor

Materials Testing

There is a wide range of **material testing** procedures that are called for in the specifications to ensure the integrity of materials, soil, and workmanship. Materials testing includes:

- Earthwork
- Concrete
- Steel and Steel Reinforcement
- Precast Concrete
- Masonry
- Fireproofing and Waterproofing
- Roofing
- Pavements
- Subgrades
- Foundations
- Non-destructive testing for welded and bolted connections, tanks and vessels.

Soil Conditions

The Agency will have engaged the services of a geotechnical engineer to determine the acceptability and suitability of soils at the construction site. The soil must be suitable to support the structures that will be constructed and supported by it. For new construction, this is usually the first interaction for quality. The site is inspected and tested to verify soil composition, gradations, moisture content and compatibility. There will be an identification of unsuitable soil material to be removed and replaced. The depth and bearing capacity of subsoil will be verified. Soils testing is performed using strength and compaction devices, sieves, scales, ovens, soil classification stations, molds, and other equipment necessary to provide moisture content, bearing ratios, density data, boring data for soils and rock, and asphalt testing.

Concrete

Testing inspections are intended to ensure that the subgrade for foundations is at the required elevation, and that the subsurface has the specified bearing capacity. Inspection of the concrete forms and their correct installation is also a function of testing and inspection, as is the proper fabrication and installation of reinforcing steel and welded wire mesh. Shop drawings submitted will be reviewed for concrete mix design and reinforcing steel to ensure compliance.

Mortar Mix

Mortar cubes used for masonry are inspected for high compressive strength, There are various types of compressive strength ranging from high to low depending on durability requirements of the specifications.

Mill Reports

Mill reports are obtained from the steel manufacturer. They are prepared at the steel mill that produces the product and contain the chemical composition of each representative sixe of rolled section produced and shipped to the steel fabricator. There must also be a certification that the steel meets the requirements of the American Institute of Steel Construction standards.

Field Welding

Field inspections of field welding includes proper alignment, placement of bolts with proper tension, and compliance with approved shop drawings.

Mechanical and Electrical Testing and Inspection

The mechanical and electrical divisions of the specifications describe required inspection and testing requirements. For example, testing for mechanical systems include air and water balancing reports, air pressure and hydrostatic pressure testing of systems, compliance with standards of various trade associations including ASHRAE, ASME, AABC and ADC.

Pre-installation Conference

Pre-installation conferences may be required in the specifications for various trades for product and installation procedure compliance. These meetings are often held for such issues as sedimentation control, cast in place work, structural steel, waterproofing of foundations, insulation, exterior wall assemblies, windows, roofing, skylights, sheet metal flashing, and architectural finishes. It is also advisable to review plans and specifications, and approved shop drawings with the contractor for such installations as elevators, millwork, fire protection systems, HVAC, electrical systems, data and communications, and security.

Sample panels and **mock-ups** are usually required when there is extensive brickwork and other decorative exterior masonry construction. A sample panel is submitted to show the intended quality of new construction. The sample panel is reviewed by the Architect, such as in a curtain wall installation. The Architect can inspect the sample and check its structural integrity, weather tightness, and other attributes before the complete construction begins. The Agency also can view the color scheme as presented in the mock-up.

Punch List

A punch list is a list of tasks which need to completed to satisfy all of the requirements of the construction contract. They are usually generated in the final phases of construction, as the Construction

Manager and the Architect/Engineer walk around the site and note down any issues and deficiencies which need to be resolved.

One would think that with a proper Quality Assurance and Quality Control program, there would be no need for a Punch List. However, it is unlikely that every single deficiency will be identified during construction, even with a very good QA/QC program in effect. The goal should be to limit the final punch list by effectively punching out the project as it progresses, to the extent possible.

The maintenance of a clean and orderly site throughout construction, as enforced by the Construction Manager, will convey quality and instills discipline. This in fact may contribute to better attention to quality and a minimal punch list at the end of the project. Pre-punching the building is an effort undertaken by the contractor and the Construction Manager. The contractor has an obligation to inspect the work of its own forces and its subcontractors as work progresses. The Construction Manager is hopefully providing full time daily inspection of work and identifying deficiencies as well. The identification of deficiencies should occur for portions of the work, and not after substantial work is completed.

Quality and Contractor Selection

Private sector clients do not need to use a low bid system and usually prefer to negotiate from a list of preferred, qualified contractors. Resorting to the lowest bidder can result in poor construction quality, if there is no means to vet the contractor who is unproven and untested by the client. Government agencies have had to struggle with the low bid system that they are often required to adhere to. Highly technical projects may have a prequalification process that restricts the bidders list to proven, experienced contractors compatible with the requirements of the project. Agencies have satisfied requirements for all qualified bidders to submit bids, and have also started to use alternative methods to select contractors, such as best value procurement, construction management at risk and competitive negotiation. Some agencies use A + B contracts that reward early completion.

Best Value Procurement

Best Value Procurement was first used by the federal government. Many states have also adopted this procurement method. In the traditional design-bid-build method, agencies have awarded contracts to the lowest responsible bidder. Payment and performance bonds guarantee that the work will be performed as promised and that subcontractors will be paid. However, in the strictest sense, government agencies only evaluate bids based on price. Best value procurement provides flexibility. In a design build procurement, there is a single source of responsibility, and prequalification processes designate acceptable bidders.

Best value procurement follows two phases. In phase one, the Agency narrows the field of potential bidders to a short list, without considering price. In phase two, the Agency selects the design-build contractor who provides based value based on technical and cost factors. The phase one process narrows the field of bidders based on technical competence and past performance. The result is a short list of contractors who are best qualified to enter into phase two and submit a bid. The final price is then negotiated.

Chapter 9 References
The following sources were utilized in writing this chapter

Fisk, E., and Rapp, R. Introduction to Engineering Construction Inspection. John Wiley & Sons. 2004 Hoboken, NJ

ISO 9000 Essentials. Retrieved from:
http://www.iso.org/iso/iso_9000_essentials

Mahoney, W. and Wetherill, E. Editors, Construction Inspection Manual. Sixth Ed. BNI Publications, Inc. Las Angeles CA

Chapter 10
Construction Safety

Construction Safety in the United States

Construction is an inherently dangerous industry. In 2002 the Bureau of Labor (BLS) Statistics reported that there were 1,225 fatal injuries in the construction sector, resulting in an accident rate of 13.3 per 100,000 workers, and an illness rate of 7.9 per 100 full time workers in the construction industry. According to the National Institute for Construction Safety and Health, over 11 million construction workers are employed in the United States, involving work at height, excavations, noise, dust, power tools, equipment, confined spaces and electricity. Construction has about 8% of U.S. workers but 22% of the fatalities - the largest number of fatalities reported for any of the industry sectors.

In 2008, ABC News reported that construction was an increasingly deadly business, especially during the building boom in the middle of the decade. In 2006, 43 workers died while performing construction in New York City, spiking fatalities 87 percent from the year before. In fact, across the United States, construction remained a dangerous business, where 20 percent of all work related fatalities occurred. Fatalities rose from 1,141 in 2003 to 2,226 in 2006. The only thing that slowed the rate of construction fatalities by 2010 was high unemployment in the industry, according to the Bureau of Labor Statistics.

Pedestrians are not immune to construction fatalities, although there are no statistics available. In Chicago in 2002, scaffolding outside the John Hancock Center plunged more than 40 floors to the ground during a windstorm, killing three women in cars.
The rise in fatalities in construction are attributed by some experts to a mix of the use of untrained immigrant workers, ignorance or

indifference to safety regulations, and contractors who cut corners in labor and material costs, compromising safety by pushing productivity by taking shortcuts.

Each year, there are nearly 6,000 workplace fatalities in the United States across all industries. There are more than 50,000 deaths attributed to workplace related illnesses. There have been more than 5.7 million non fatal injuries in the workplace that cost United States businesses over $125 billion annually. It has been reported by the BLS that the major cause of death and injury on a construction site is a result of falls from height, electrocution, being struck by equipment, being caught between equipment, and trench excavation cave ins.

OSHA Standards for Safety

The Occupational Health and Safety Act and the administrators for the Act, the Occupational Health and Safety Administration (OSHA) have developed OSHA Standards that address these major hazards, and other hazards that workers encounter on a construction site. If the Agency uses a Construction Manager or Resident Engineer for its project, they will be the agent for determining if the contractors that are working under their direction are implementing a compliant health and safety program in their respective operations, and are complying with applicable OSHA regulations and the approved construction safety program submitted by the contractor. The OSHA regulations are a compilation of mandatory standards for occupational safety and health. The regulations also require a reporting and recordkeeping system to monitor job related illnesses, injuries and fatalities, and also requires training and other support programs. OSHA has been credited with reducing annual workforce fatalities by more than 50 percent, and work place injuries by 40 percent. Trenching and excavation fatalities have been reduced by more than 25 percent. The OSHA Standards are focused on prevention of injuries that result from the following hazards, which are the most frequently reported job related accidents: Falls from elevated areas: Being struck by an object or machine / equipment; Being caught in between; and electrical hazards.

Obligations Under OSHA

Employers have obligations to meet OSHA standards, including:

- Providing a safe and healthful workplace free of recognized hazards
- Following the requirements of OSHA standards
- Providing appropriate training to employees
- Maintaining recordkeeping of work related illnesses and injuries
- Cooperating with OSHA inspectors
- Posting OSHA posters and submitting an annual summary of work related illnesses and injuries

Workers also have obligations under OSHA. Employees must:

- Follow employer safety and health rules and the construction safety plan, as approved
- Wear or use required protective gear and safety equipment
- Follow safe work practices as directed
- Report hazardous conditions to a supervisor or safety inspector
- Report hazardous conditions to OSHA if they continue after they are identified
- Cooperate with OSHA inspectors who come on site
- Obtain proper training including OSHA 10 hour and 30 hour training

Common Violations Issued by OSHA

OSHA issues violations for non compliance with OSHA regulations. Not all violations are the result of dangerous or hazardous job site conditions. Some violations are issued because contractors have failed to comply with reporting and posting requirements. Paperwork violations include:

- Failure to provide the Log and Summary of Occupational Injuries and Illnesses forms properly updated
- Failure to adhere to the OSHA General Duty Clause of the regulations
- Failure to report a fatality and multiple hospitalization incidents

- Failure to record and report occupational injuries and illness on required forms

Top Ten Violations Cited for Non-compliance with OSHA Standards

#1. Failure to guard open sided floors and platforms. Standard: 500 (d) 1(1) Fall Protection

#2. Failure to protect against impact, falling and flying objects to protect against head injuries. Standard: 100 (a). Personal Protective Equipment (PPE).

#3. Failure to provide electrical ground fault protection. Standard 404(b)(1)(i). Electrical.

#4. Path to ground is missing or discontinuous. Standard: 404(f)(6). Electrical

#5. Failure to install protective systems at excavations and trenches. Standard: 652 (a)(1). Trench and Excavation Protective Systems

#6. Violation of Guardrail specifications for tubular frame scaffolds. Standard: 451 (d)(10). Scaffolding

#7. Misuse or non-use of Personal Protective Equipment for specific construction operations. Standard: 28 (a) PPE

#8. Improper or missing stair rails for riser elevations. Standard: 1052 (c)(1).

#9. Lack of Approved containers or tanks for flammable or combustible liquid storage. Standard: 152(1)(1). Fire Protection.

#10. Violations in general housekeeping requirements. Standard: Section: 25(a). General Provisions.

Key OSHA Standards and Requirements

General Duty Clause

When the OSHA standards were enacted, it was understood that it would be impossible to foresee and create a standard for every possible hazard in the workplace, so they created a section to the law requiring employers to protect against any foreseeable hazards not covered by specific OSHA regulation. Section (5)(a)(1) of OSHA states that each employer must furnish a place of employment that is free from recognized hazards that are causing or are likely to cause death or serious physical harm to employees.

For a hazard to be covered by the general duty clause it must be "recognized." OSHA will determine whether a particular hazard is recognized on a case-by-case basis. Some critics argue that this criterion is based on an objective and not a subjective standard. In other words, the question of whether a hazard is recognized is determined by looking not simply at what the employer actually recognized but what it *should have* recognized. The basis for a finding, therefore is: actual recognition of the hazard by the employer; recognition of the hazard by the employer's industry; and common sense.

Generally, OSHA standards for all worksites require:

- Emergency action and fire prevention plans
- Access by employees to exposure and medical records maintained by the employer
- Hazard Communication for hazardous materials
- Injury and illness prevention programs
- Safety standards that apply must be known by workers
- Lift slab operations, concrete and masonry

Equipment and Materials
Unsafe equipment and materials must be tagged, locked or have controls removed, including machinery, tools, material and equipment. Equipment may only be operated by trained and qualified employees.

Fire Prevention
The employer must develop effective fire prevention and protection programs.

First Aid and Medial Attention
Procedures for first aid and medical attention must be in place including first aid supplies and hospital contact information.

Housekeeping

Proper containers must be provided for collection and separation of waste. Combustible scrap and debris must be removed at regular intervals. Every building or structure must have means of egress free of debris.

Hazardous Communications Requirements

Regulations concerning **hazardous substances and communications** are found in the General Duty Clause, and in other OSHA subparts. In OSHA Subpart Z, toxic substances such as asbestos are identified, and exposure limits, compliance requirements, hazardous operations, monitoring procedures, emergency situations, and training requirements are provided. Subpart D of the OSHA regulations requires a system for hazardous communication. Each worksite requires a written hazardous communications program that includes the following:

- A list of hazardous chemicals known to be present
- Communicating hazards by employers for non-routine tasks
- Material Safety Data Sheets (MSDS) provide workers and emergency personnel with proper procedures for handling or working with particular substances. This includes health effects, first aid, storage, disposal, protective equipment, etc.

Competent Person

OSHA General Health and Safety provisions require the designation by contractors of a competent person to conduct frequent and regular inspections. This person does not have to consult the contract Project Manager for permission to take decisive action if there is a health or safety violation or threat, and must take prompt action to eliminate the threat. Competent Person standards cover:

- General safety and health
- Lead
- Hearing protection
- Rigging equipment for material handling
- Material hoists and personnel hoists
- Excavations and protective systems, soil classifications
- Steel erection

- Welding, cutting and heating preservative coatings
- Wiring
- Scaffolds
- Cranes and derricks
- Underground construction
- Demolition and blasting
- Asbestos
- Fall protection
- Stairways and ladders

Material Handling

The OSHA standard for material handling is found in 29CFR 1926 Subpart H. This standard addresses handling and storing materials such as hoisting steel, transporting concrete blocks with trucks, carrying bags, stacking materials manually, and material storage. The standards address safe handling manually and with machinery, including forklifts, cranes, rigging, bulldozers and other heavy equipment. It prescribes inspection if items such as chains and slings used in hoisting, and the safe storage of materials on the project site.

Electrical Hazards

The OSHA standards for **Electrical** are found in 29CFR 1926 Subpart K. Other applicable standards include the **National Institute of Occupational Safety and Health (NISOH)** and **National Electrical Code (NEC)**. The regulations identify terms such as electric current, circuit, resistance, conductors, and grounding. Employees at construction sites are exposed to electric shock, burns, fires, and explosions. The standards are designed to minimize potential hazards. 12 percent of young worker work place fatalities are caused by accidents that involve electricity. Accidents are usually caused by unsafe equipment, improper electrical installation, and unsafe work practices. Internal body fluids, unfortunately, are great conductors of electricity, and there is little resistance to the flow of current upon contact with an electrical source. Most fatal electrical shocks travel through the heart. Inspections for electrical safety and prevention of accidents focuses on inadequate wiring, ground fault circuit interruptors designed to direct electricity to the ground as a safety measure, poorly insulated wires, ungrounded electrical systems or tools, damaged tools and equipment, the use of improper personal protective equipment, the danger of overhead power lines, and wet conditions.

Excavations

The OSHA standards for **Excavations** are found in 29CFR 1926 Subpart P. There are many hazards to workers posed by construction excavation operations. These include cave-ins, asphyxiation due to lack of oxygen in a confined space, drowning, and the inhalation of toxic fumes. OSHA regulations are designed to protect workers in excavations and trenches. Basically, these standards require that walls and faces of excavations where workers are exposed to danger by moving ground be guarded by shoring systems, safe sloping of the ground, trench shields and boxes, or other means. They also provide requirements for moving machinery on the ground near excavations, to avoid collapse. Excavation and trenching are among the most hazardous of construction operations. Most accidents occur in trenches that are only 5- 15 feet deep.

Fall Protection

The OSHA standards for **Fall Protection** are found in 29CFR 1926 Subpart M. OSHA standards in Subpart M and elsewhere identify areas and activities where fall protection is needed. It clarifies what an employer must do to provide fall protection for employees, including the identification of fall hazards, and requires training programs to protect against these hazards. Falls are the leading cause of death in the construction industry. Most fatalities occur when workers fall from open-sided floors or through floor openings. A fall from as little as four feet can cause death. Open sided floors and platforms six feet in height must be guarded. Fall protection equipment includes body support for the work application, connecting to secure areas with lanyards and snap hooks, anchorage systems for safe connections, safety nets, guard rails, and other means.

Personal Protective Equipment

The OSHA standards for **Personal Protective Equipment (PPE)** are found in 29CFR 1926 Subpart I. OSHA addresses three basic means to protect workers. When we see workers donning PPE, we might think that PPE is the primary way to protect workers. In fact, it is the last resort in protecting workers, although PPE is a very important and protectoral defense against hazards/ OSHA teaches prevention as the first line of defense through engineering and administrative controls. *Engineering Controls* and *Administrative Controls* – methods that employers can implement to reduce or eliminate a particular workplace hazard — must always be considered first when evaluating and mitigating workplace hazards.

The basic concept behind *engineering controls* is that, to the extent feasible, the work environment and the job itself should be designed to eliminate hazards or reduce exposure to hazards. Engineering controls are based on the following principles: If feasible, design the facility, equipment, or process to remove the hazard or substitute something that is not hazardous. If removal is not feasible, enclose the hazard to prevent exposure in normal operations. Where complete enclosure is not feasible, establish barriers or local ventilation to reduce exposure to the hazard in normal operations. Examples of engineering controls would be to control the inhalation of dust particles by workers by installing exhaust systems or wetting systems. Another example is to prefabricate components at ground level rather than at height and then hoist into place, to reduce fall hazards from working at height.

While safe work practices can be considered forms of *administrative controls*, OSHA uses the term administrative controls to mean other measures aimed at reducing employee exposure to hazards. These measures include additional relief workers, exercise breaks and rotation of workers. These types of controls are normally used in conjunction with other controls that more directly prevent or control exposure to the hazard.
If PPE is to be used, a PPE program should be implemented. This program should address the hazards present; the selection, maintenance, and use of PPE; the training of employees; and monitoring of the program to ensure its ongoing effectiveness. Protective equipment, including personal protective equipment for eyes, face, head, and extremities, protective clothing, respiratory devices, and protective shields and barriers, shall be provided, used, and maintained in a sanitary and reliable condition wherever it is necessary by reason of hazards of processes or environment, chemical hazards, radiological hazards, or mechanical irritants encountered in a manner capable of causing injury or impairment in the function of any part of the body through absorption, inhalation or physical contact.

Scaffolding

The OSHA standards for **Scaffolding** are found in 29CFR 1926 Subpart L. The regulations require that the erection of scaffolds meet the requirements of the OSHA standards for scaffold erection. The thrust of the OSHA standard is to protect workers from fall protection, and being struck by objects from height. The regulations establish fall protection requirements. These include requirements for guardrail heights, safe means of access and fall protection for the erection and dismantling of scaffolds. The standards require continuous inspection by a competent person, employee training, standards for the structural integrity of scaffolds, including footings and anchorage for scaffolds; capacity for carrying maximum intended loads. The standards prohibit the placing of unstable objects to support the scaffold or planks; guardrails and toe-boards on open sides and ends of platforms.

Cranes, Derricks and Hoist Safety

The OSHA standards for **Cranes, Derricks and Hoists** are found in 29CFR 1926 Subpart N. Crane, derrick, and hoist safety hazards are addressed in specific standards for the construction industry. The employer must comply with the manufacturer's specifications and limitations applicable to the operation of any and all cranes and derricks. Where manufacturer's specifications are not available, the limitations assigned to the equipment shall be based on the determinations of a qualified engineer competent in this field, with appropriate documentation. The regulations require that rated load capacities, recommended operating speeds, special hazard warnings, or instruction, are conspicuously posted on all equipment. Instructions or warnings must be visible to the operator while he is at his control station. The regulations require that the employer designate a competent person who shall inspect all machinery and equipment prior to each use, and during use, to make sure it is in safe operating condition. Any deficiencies shall be repaired, or defective parts replaced, before continued use. The standards require that a thorough, annual inspection of the hoisting machinery shall be made by a competent person, or by a government or private agency recognized by the U.S. Department of Labor. The employer shall maintain a record of the dates and results of inspections for each hoisting machine and piece of equipment.

Stairways and Ladders

The OSHA standards for **Stairways and Ladders** are found in 29CFR 1926 Subparts X. There are also applicable standards in Subparts L (Scaffolds) and M (Fall Protection). Working on and around stairways and ladders is hazardous. Stairways and ladders are major sources of injuries and fatalities among construction workers. OSHA rules apply to all stairways and ladders used in construction, alteration, repair, painting, decorating and demolition of worksites covered by OSHA's construction safety and health standards. The OSHA standards provide for the use of temporary stairs, including elevation breaks, requirements for landings, and the use handrails and midrails to protect against falls, and requirements for free access by workers. The standards also define requirements for the use of ladders, regulations for different types of ladders, and the safe use of ladders including inspection for condition.

OSHA Inspections

OSHA has the right to perform unannounced worksite inspections. The can be routine, or in response to urgency, imminent danger, fatalities and accidents in the past, employee complaints, and other reasons.

When the OSHA Compliance Inspector arrives, the Construction Manager at the project site should greet the OSHA inspector, check credentials, and assign a representative to walk the site. The contractor's safety representatives should also be invited on the walk around. The OSHA inspector has the right to walk the site if there is no management representative present.

There will be an opening conference, allowing more information concerning the inspection process. The inspector should explain the nature of the visit and the scope of the inspection along with standards that apply. If the inspection was triggered by an employee complaint, a copy of the complaint should be produced on request. The inspector will likely not reveal the name of the employee who filed the complaint.

If there is no authorized employee representative the inspector will consult with a reasonable amount of workers concerning health and safety issues in the workplace. These consultations are usually held privately. The inspector may request reports of work-related injuries and/or accidents recorded in the project OSHA log. The Construction Manager must be prepared to show the compliance inspector the contractor safety program, hazard communication program, and other records relating to the safety of your employees.

The OSHA inspector decides the route and scope of the inspection. The inspector will closely monitor conditions, speak with workers and make a photographic record. The Construction Manager should record conditions with a camera and take notes.

At the closing conference, the OSHA inspector and the Construction Manager will discuss all unsafe conditions observed during the inspection with the employer. The inspector will clearly indicate all violations for which a safety citation can be issued. At this point in time, the employer is made aware of appeal rights by the OSHA Inspector. The inspector will not indicate any proposed penalties due to the fact that only the OSHA area director is authorized to do this, and not the inspector.
The Construction Manager should be given a chance to discuss these violations, presenting the other side of the case, as applicable. It would be helpful to produce, at this time, evidence of compliance efforts and provide information that may help OSHA decide the amount of time necessary to correct alleged violations. The policy of the Agency should be full cooperation with OSHA. They are most likely at the site because of a question about safety at the site. The objective is to correct safety violations and provide a safe working environment at your project site.

Citations may be issued by OSHA inspectors due to violation of OSHA standards. Citations are posted by the inspector with the proposed length of time required to correct the violation. Employers have the right to appeal actions by OSHA inspectors before an administrative law judge.

Commitment to Safety

The Agency no doubt has placed a high priority on safety for every project that it administers and manages. No project can be considered a success if it is conducted in a way that disregards safety. In such an environment, there can be no discipline, no regard for standards, and no respect for the Agency. A project that disregards safety is not likely to produce a quality product because standards are not considered important enough to be adhered to. An agency that only pays lip service to safety and does not require safety to filter down from the top is not able to run safe projects. Workers at a site where safety is not strictly enforced become lax. They know there is no commitment from the top. They stop wearing hard hats and other safety equipment. They may even smoke on the site regardless of the types of materials being stored. Housekeeping becomes sloppy, and there is debris that pose additional hazards.

The contractors that work for the Agency need to clearly define their commitment to safety, the policies concerning safety, and be able to show how they have invested in developing a culture of safety on their jobs. The commitment to safety must come from the top. From there, line management is responsible for carrying out the safety program.

Weekly toolbox safety talk sessions are usually conducted at the job site. They usually do not last more than 15 minutes, and are held in order to discuss specific work tasks and reminders of potential hazards that may be encountered during the performance of these tasks. Employees who attend should sign in to indicate that they have attended the session.

Typically, companies will have a system to enforce the safety program. This may include a warning notification system. After a series of warnings to an employee who consistently violates safety rules for the project, they have become a serious liability and threat to themselves, their coworkers and other personnel at the project site. The safety program will not be taken seriously on your project site if there are no consequences. If the contractor is unwilling to terminate employees who flagrantly disregard safety, the Agency's Construction Manager, and the Agency itself should not tolerate the continued presence of workers with no regard for safety, and insist that they be removed from your project site.

Contractor Safety Plan

Before a job starts, there must be a job specific **safety plan** that is developed. A written contractor safety plan establishes requirements for construction operations on your project site. They are designed to provide a safe working environment, and ensures that the contractor's employees are trained to protect themselves from existing and potential hazards, and to protect non construction personnel, pedestrians and the traveling public from the hazards of your operations on site.

The major components of a contractor's safety plan should include the following:

- Requirements for personnel protective equipment and first aid equipment
- Requirements for formal training programs

- Procedures for emergency evacuation of employees who are injured on the job
- Safety record and accident report requirements
- Site safety inspections.

A project specific safety program may include but is not limited to the following topics:

- Accountability for the safety program
- Pre-project planning for safety
- Communication requirements for the safety program
- Training of personnel
- Identification of contractor safety representative / safety manager
- Emergency contact information
- Plan for safety orientation and safety toolbox meetings
- Contractor hazard assessment based on scope of work analysis
- Accident reporting and investigation procedures including "near miss" reporting
- Fire Protection and prevention
- Hazardous Materials handling
- Property protection and damage procedures
- Weather related emergencies
- Hazardous communication including hazardous substance identification, lock out and tag out procedures
- Safety audits and inspections
- Noncompliance procedures
- Engineering, administrative and personnel protective equipment controls
- Respiratory protection
- Fall protection and prevention
- Scaffolds
- Excavation and trenching
- Electrical

- Housekeeping and sanitation
- Cranes and Lifts
- Rigging
- Steel Erection
- Ladders and Stairs
- Mobile Equipment
- Motorized Equipment
- Hand and Power Tools
- Barriers, barricades and safety tape
- Maintenance and protection of traffic
- Signage
- Visitors
- Security
- Employee Conduct

The Safety and Health Manager

The Contractor should have a competent person that is designated as the safety and health manager assigned to the project. This is not usually a full time safety position unless specifically required by the contract, That person is responsible for:

- The administration and dissemination of company safety and loss control information and procedures
- Monitoring compliance by employees with the approved safety and health plan
- The authority to order a work suspension if there are threats of imminent danger and safety hazards

Depending on the size of the project and the policy of the Agency, the Construction Manager may be funded to provide a part time or full time Safety Engineer who will monitor contractor compliance with the approved safety program.

Some agencies with very large capital programs, such as the New York City Department of Environmental Protection, have engaged safety and environmental health consultants to provide health and safety audits of their entire multi-billion dollar capital program, monitoring not only the safety compliance of general contractors, but of Resident Engineers and Construction Managers who are also responsible for monitoring safety on a full time basis.

Safety by Design

Construction remains the most dangerous industry for workers, who suffer illness, injury, and death in far greater proportions than other industries. Traditionally, safety in construction is the primary responsibility of general contractors and subcontractors, and not designers and Construction Managers. Data collection through a literature search, review of OSHA regulations, and review of health and safety statistics indicate that construction safety is substantially improved when qualified designers practice Safety by Design. Safety is enhanced when Construction Managers perform design review and constructability review in the design phase of a project, with the objective of building safety into the design. There is some resistance to the implementation of **Safety by Design** in the United States. Resistance may be overcome through an emphasis on training and education, Safety in Design awareness, changes in perceptions and practices in professional liability insurance, and a rethinking of the emphasis of safety responsibility in the OSHA and other applicable safety regulations.

Safety by Design is an effort that is made in the design phase of a construction project to consider the safety of workers who will be constructing the project. In the United States, such a focus on worker safety in the early stages of a project is neither a part of the traditional aspects of design nor a part of the traditional aspects of construction safety practices. The focus of designers is on the safety of the end users of the facility: its occupants, its maintenance personnel, and the public who utilize the facility, and not the worker who builds it. There are reasons why construction worker safety has not been addressed adequately in project design. Construction safety requirements fall primarily on general contractors and subcontractors. The safety emphasis is on the means and methods practiced in the construction phase. Perhaps there are other effective ways of addressing construction safety, in addition to proactive safety management during construction. The key to improving construction safety is to make the working environment safer before construction begins.

Safety by Design as a concept has not fully taken hold in this country for various reasons: (a) The Occupational Safety and Health Administration (OSHA) through its regulations and enforcement, places responsibility for safety on the general contractor and subcontractor and not for designers; (b) The education and training of designers limits their ability to perform Safety in Design; (c) There is a lack of Safety in Design tools, guidelines, and procedures; (d) Designers are not fully integrated on the project team after the finalization of design documents; (e) Traditionally, designers do not view their role as promoting construction worker safety since this is in the bailiwick of the contractor; and (f) Concerns about professional liability although there still remains associated liability. The OSHA regulations (OSHA 20 CFR 1926.16c) state that "In no case shall the prime contractor be relieved of overall responsibility for compliance with the requirements of this part.

The United Kingdom (U.K.), Australia, and some other countries moved away from reliance solely on contractors for safety responsibility when they implemented their respective regulations placing Safety in Design responsibilities on architects and engineers. In the U.K., design engineers are required by law to specify in detail, the safety of construction workers in their design. The Australian government has also taken a leadership role in requiring design in construction. There are a number of ways that the Safety by Design paradigm can shift in the United States. This requires a different approach to safety by architects, engineers and construction managers. It also requires a change in the perspective of private and public Owners. There are many human and financial cost benefits to the practice of Safety by Design, and Owners need to understand that these benefits outweigh the additional costs that are incurred in design to implement safety before construction.

In the U.K, where the government has promulgated regulations to require that designers incorporate safety into their design for construction, statistics released by the Health and Safety Executive (HSE) for 2005/06 show the rate of fatal and major injuries in the construction industry is continuing to fall. An analysis of fatal injuries reported in the U.K. for the construction industry in the years ranging from 1981, when the CDM regulations were not in effect, and 2008/2009 shows a downward trend since their introduction. Although these statistics are not conclusive, it is instructive to note that construction in the U.K. continues to have the largest incidence of fatal injuries of the main industry groups. In 2008/2009, there were 53 fatal injuries, or 2.5 per 100,000 workers.

The rate of fatal injuries in construction over the past decade has trended downward. In a comparable period in 2000/2001, there were

5.9 fatal injuries per 100,000 workers in construction, and in the past three years the rate declined a total of 34 percent. The reports of fatal injuries have steadily fallen, but the rate of major injury is still the highest among the U.K.'s industries at 254.1 per 100,000 employees. This is an indication that the resources must be provided to the HSE for the full enforcement of the CDM regulations, and that education and training to promote the benefits of compliance needs to be continued.

The Best Practices models guide designers in making choices which still allow design objectives for the project to be met, but with promoting safety as well. The principles of the Best Practices for Safety in Design start with the premise that persons in control of design decisions are best able to promote health and safety in the preconstruction stages. Safe design must apply to the project life cycle, from conception to demolition. Following are some examples of "Best Practices" in the pro-active design for safety:

1. Prefabricated Components - The design of prefabricated components reduces the number of activities that must be performed at heights and therefore reduces the risk of fall related and struck by related injuries.

2. Electrical Hazards - The contract specifications can specify the crane radii and sufficient vertical space required that is clear of obstructions such as overhead power lines, a major source of accidents when cranes come into contact with energized lines. In fact, electrical hazards are reduced or eliminated by requiring in the design the disconnection, reduction of voltage ore re-routing of power lines around the project site before work begins. Existing power lines can be located on contract drawings, in relation to the new structure, as well.

3. Placement of Openings on Roofs and Floors - By considering where openings on roofs and floors are placed, structural designers can influence project safety by placing openings of roof skylights away from readily accessed areas by construction workers in proximity of the openings, to prevent falls and drop hazards. Other design solutions include the installation of permanent guardrails around skylights; the design of domed skylights instead of flat ones; furnishing skylights with shatterproof or shatter resistant glass; and designed skylight installation on raised curbs.

4. Use trench-less technology to eliminate hazards that result from trenching – Trenchless technology replaces the need for open cut excavation and conventional trenching methods through tunneling, drilling and boring methods that minimally disrupt surface areas, and eliminate backfilling, compaction and restoration of ground surfaces, along with the material and labor costs associated with conventional methods. Safety impacts include eliminating hazards for fall protection, cave-ins, and equipment operation hazards.

5. Primers and Sealer Specifications - Specify primers and sealers that do not emit noxious fumes. This reduces illnesses caused by contact or inhalation of toxic fumes.

6. Fire Safety - Schedule the underground firewater system to be constructed early in the construction phase. Similarly, in high-rise construction, schedule the firewater protection system to be operational early in the construction phase. Permanent emergency exit signs should be required to be erected as early as possible.

Chapter 10 References
The following sources were utilized in writing this chapter

OSHA Standards for the Construction Industry. U.S. Department of Labor. Occupational Safety & Health Administration. Retrieved from: http://www.osha.gov

MacCollum, D. Construction Safety Engineering Principles. 2997. McGraw-Hill Companies. New York, NY

Palumbo, A. "Safety in Design". Enhancing Construction Safety by Implementing Safety in the Design Phase. 2010. CM EJournal. Construction Management Association of America. Retrieved from: http://cmaanet.org/cm-ejournal

Al Palumbo

Chapter 11
Sustainability

Sustainable Development

What is Sustainability?

Sustainability refers to the policies and strategies that meet society's present needs without compromising the ability of future generations to meet their own needs. For public administrators of construction, the challenges going forward are to develop and implement strategies, policies, and practices needed to advance sustainability. The challenges will present themselves through far sighted initiatives, legislation, evolving building code requirements, and through the executive orders of government officials. There are drivers that will induce government to embrace sustainability to greater levels than present. This will derive from the necessity to reduce waste and pollution, conserve natural resources including water and energy sources, and rising costs that result in scarcity of energy sources. Developments in science and technology will also drive change. Traditionally, construction has not focused on the long term impacts it has on the environment. Many practices in this regard are wasteful and inefficient in the manner of the use of land and natural resources. Progress has been made toward achieving "sustainable development".

Sustainable development

Sustainable development is a relatively new term that emerged from the conservation movement of the 1970's in response to concerns about how human decisions affect the earth's environment. Sustainable development has different meanings to different groups, but the most accepted definition was derived from the Brundtland Commission Report of 1987. The report addressed long-term environmental strategies for achieving sustainable development in the future. It defined sustainable development as meeting the needs for the present without compromising the ability of future generations to meet their own needs. Simply stated, the decisions that we make today to use our forests, water, minerals and other natural resources must take into account how these resources are used and processed, and for whom. Will the resources that are left for future generations and the environment be sufficient to meet the needs of future generations?

The construction industry is a great consumer of natural resources, consuming approximately 40% of extracted resources, and about 40% of generated energy in the industrial nations. As development continues, concerns about the impact of unsustainable development without considering long term impacts have resulted in public policies for sustainability. Physical construction activity has had negative impacts on the environment's natural systems, including animal and plant life, water resources, the release of pollutants including toxins, the disruption of natural drainage systems, and the generation of solid waste. Buildings require a vast amount of materials. They require land to be sited on. They will cycle energy and water throughout their life span. Public agencies, by sustaining sustainable development, take up the challenge of building beneficial public works with minimal damage to the environment, not only during construction, but in the operation and maintenance, and the ultimate demolition of the structures that they build.

Sustainability and Public Projects

Municipalities nationwide have launched sustainability initiatives for their capital projects. For example:

- In 2006 the Portland Oregon City Council adopted a resolution to create the "Sustainable City Government Partnership". The intent was to establish a citywide collaboration to integrate sustainable practices and efficient use of resources into municipal operations. The initiative has resulted in requiring public agencies in the city to make city operations more cost effective and resource efficient, down to the installation of solar powered parking meters.
- On Earth Day in 2007, New York City's Mayor Michael Bloomberg announced Plan NYC for a "greener greater New York" geared to the reduction of carbon emissions.
- The Sustainable Jersey Program encouraged New Jersey municipalities in the creation of sustainable communicates under a sustainable grant program.
- Colorado and other states have encouraged and assisted in the development of sustainable communities in cities like Denver.

The acknowledgment of the need to embrace sustainability by government has evolved over the past two decades. Agenda 21 was a plan of action that was endorsed by 178 counties at the United Nations Conference on Environment and Development, also known as the June, 1992 Earth Summit, espousing the following principles on sustainability: (1). The right to development must be fulfilled in such a way that it equitably meets developmental and environmental needs of present and future generations; and (2). In order to achieve sustainable development, environmental protection must be integral to the development process, and cannot be isolated from development. Other initiatives followed, but on national and international levels, the world has not reached levels of sustainability that can critically address energy use, greenhouse gas emission reduction, and the protection of the ecosystem.

Regulations Affecting Construction

There are numerous existing statues and mandates that support sustainability. Many practices, existing facilities and new construction projects are subject to the **Clean Water Act (CWA)**, the Resource Conservation and Recovery Act (RCRA), the Toxic Substances Control Act (TSCA), the Federal Insecticide, Fungicide and Rodenticide Act (FIFRA), the Energy Policy Act of 2005, and many others.

Government policies, regulations and incentives will continue to make sustainability operational. The **National Environmental Protection Act of 1969 (NEPA)** which predates the U.S. Environmental Protection Agency, requires that the federal government, in partnership with state government, use "all practical means and measures....to create and maintain conditions under which man and nature can exist in productive harmony, and fulfill the social, economic and other requirements of present and future generations of Americans."

Land Use, Planning and Zoning

Land use typical refers to the way in which activities are distributed across space, including such factors as location and density of these activities, such as residential, office, commercial, industrial and other activities. This also applies to transportation systems, including the physical infrastructure of roads, highways, bridges, sidewalks, rail systems, etc. and the levels of service that is determined by traffic levels and other factors.

Rules and regulations govern density and the intensity of development. Density measures the amount of activity that can be found in an area, whether the measurement is population, employment, or building square footage per unit of area. It is measured in terms of people per square acre, jobs per square mile, or building square footage. It sets parameters for the ratio between floor space in a building and the size of the parcel where the building sits. Federal, state, and local governments regulate growth and development through laws that are enacted and regulations that are promulgated.

Local Zoning Laws

Zoning laws provide mechanisms for the regulation of land use. Zoning shapes the city, town, neighborhood, or jurisdiction. Zoning laws determine the size and use of buildings, where they can be located, and how dense an area will be allowed to become. Permitted land use is determined in geographic areas and allows planning policies that take into account economic growth, quality of life and the environment.

Zoning practices sometimes resulted in a strict segregation of land use. In some jurisdictions, zoning has become more flexible in accommodating a mix of uses, particularly in urban areas that have created new urban streetscapes and has helped to revitalize neighborhoods.

Zoning districts are typically divided into three basic categories: residential, commercial, and manufacturing. These are further subdivided into lower, medium, and higher density districts. Each zoning district regulates:

- Permitted uses
- The size of the building in relation to the size of the zoning lot, or floor area ratio (FAR)
- For residential units, the number of dwelling spaces permitted, the amount of open space required on the zoning lot and the maximum amount of the lot that can be covered by a building (lot coverage)
- The distance between the building and the front, side, and rear
- The amount of parking required
- Other features that apply to the type of construction allowed in the district

Environmental Laws

The National Environmental Policy Act (NEPA) requires federal agencies to ensure that environmental factors are considered in decision making, to mitigate environmental impacts and identify reasonable alternatives. The NEPA requires the development of an Environmental Impact Statement (EIS) where proposed activities will have a significant affect on the quality of the human environment. This document addresses positive as well as negative environmental effects, and usually lists alternative actions that can be taken.

Several state governments require a document that is similar to the EIS that must be submitted to the state for certain actions. One example are laws that were enacted in New York State that require that most projects or activities proposed by a state agency to prepare an EIS in accordance with its State Environmental Quality Review (SEQR). SEQR requires these agencies to identify and mitigate the significant environmental impacts of the project that is being proposed.

The Federal Water Pollution Control Act, also referred to as the "Clean Water Act", was a comprehensive piece of legislation with the goal of restoring and maintaining the biological, physical and chemical integrity of the nation's waters. It originally was enacted in 1948, was frequently amended and then reorganized in 1972, and has continued to be amended. The Act required comprehensive programs for eliminating and reducing pollution of interstate waters and tributaries and improving the sanitary condition of groundwater and surface water. The U.S. Environmental Protection Agency (EPA) enforces the Clean Water Act. State water quality standards are required, including permits for discharge of pollutants into navigable waters. States are funded through the EPA for their water quality programs.

The Army Corps of Engineers issues permits under EPA guidelines, known as Section 404 permitting, for the disposal of dredged and fill materials into navigable waterways and wetlands.

Superfund and Brownfield Development

Superfund and Brownfield Sites

Superfund refers to an environmental program that was established to address abandoned hazardous waste sites. It was established by the **Comprehensive Environmental Response, Compensation and Liability Act of 1980, as amended (CERCLA).** The law was enacted after the discovery of toxic waste dumps such as the Love Canal in the 1970s. It allows the EPA to clean up these sites and compel the responsible polluters to perform cleanups and reimburse the government for costs it incurs in the cleanup of these sites. The Superfund cleanup process assesses sites, places them on the National Priorities List, and establishes and develops cleanup plans. The process involves the states, and ensures community involvement.

Brownfield Sites refer to land that has been abandoned or underutilized industrial and commercial sites that may be available for redevelopment. The land may be contaminated by hazardous waste or pollution, but if cleaned up, can potentially be redeveloped. Superfund sites have concentrations of hazardous waster or pollution that is considered too high for Brownfield development.

The redevelopment of Brownfields turns unproductive land into productive land, and has factored into programs sponsored by federal, state and local government for economic development projects using Brownfields. At the federal level, the U.S. Economic Development Administration has encouraged Brownfields reuse through grants, planning and technical assistance, revolving loan fund capitalization, infrastructure construction and other programs. State and local governments have in turn developed programs for the new development of these sites.

Best Management Practices (BMP)

Best Management Practices have been developed and are often required to provide structural and engineered control systems and devices to treat polluted storm water and to protect wetlands and waterways from pollutants carried by storm water, through storm water management practices. These practices are put into affect in the construction of heavy infrastructure projects such as roadways, mass transit, sewer and water main installations, and site development for new construction. Examples of storm water management and BMP include:

- Management of storm water to control flooding and erosion
- Control of hazardous materials to prevent release of pollutants into the environment
- Management of storm water systems to remove contaminants before they pollute surface or groundwater sources
- Construction of structures such as ponds, swales and wetlands to work with existing drainage systems.

Leadership in Energy and Environmental Design (LEED)

The public sector is increasingly embracing sustainability, and many current design and construction management solicitations now address goals for **Leadership in Energy and Environmental Design (LEED)**. The LEED initiative promotes green building by providing verification that a building was designed and constructed with a goal that was met during construction to improve performance, measured in water efficiency, energy efficiency, carbon dioxide emissions, improved indoor environmental quality, and the strategic use of resources and the effort to control their impacts in a positive way. The **U.S. Green Building Council (USGBC)** developed LEED to provide designer, Owners, constructors and operators with the basis for implementing green building design, construction, maintenance and operations. The Green Building Certification Institute (GBCI) was founded by USGBC to provide a means to let building professionals become LEED Accredited. The accreditations include LEED Accredited Professional (LEED AP), LEED Green Associate (LEED GA), and third party certifications for projects that are seeking LEED certification.

The GBCI describes construction project LEED Certification on its website in detail. To summarize the process, certification provides an "independent, third party verification" that a building project meets the highest green building performance measures. LEED certification has international recognition as the standard that a project that is environmentally responsible.

LEED certification provides environmental benefits and is financially beneficial in the long run, to the owner by:

- Lowering operating costs and increasing asset value
- Reducing waste sent to landfills
- Conserving energy and water
- Developing healthier and safer buildings for occupants
- Creating compact and walkable communities with good access to neighborhood amenities and transit
- Protecting natural resources and farmland by encouraging growth to be located in areas with existing infrastructure
- Reducing harmful greenhouse gas emissions
- Qualifying for tax rebates, zoning allowances, and other incentives in hundreds of cities
- Demonstrating an Owner's commitment to environmental stewardship and social responsibility

LEED Ratings are used to determine LEED Certification. They are based on goals and accomplishments in the following major areas:

- Planning and project location
- Sustainable sites
- Efficient use of water resources
- Energy and atmosphere
- Materials and resources
- Indoor environmental quality
- Innovation and design process
- Regional priority

The certification level depends on the number of points the building is awarded in five distinct categories. These categories are designed to take into account the different aspects of a green building. A summary of areas leading to **LEED certification** follows by category. These were in effect in 2011:

Indoor Environmental Quality
A maximum of 15 points are devoted to this criteria. A project can receive points for establishing good indoor air quality. The project demonstrates that it can eliminate, reduce and manage sources of indoor air pollution, ensure thermal comfort and control of thermostat systems, and provide connections to the outdoor environment. One point is assigned to each of the following checklist items established for this category:

- Outdoor air delivery monitoring
- Increased ventilation
- Construction indoor air quality (IAQ) management plan, during construction
- Construction IAQ management plan, before occupancy
- Low-Emitting materials, adhesives & sealants
- Low-Emitting materials, paints & coatings
- Low-Emitting materials, carpet systems
- Low-Emitting materials, composite wood & Agrifiber products
- Indoor chemical & pollutant source control
- Controllability of systems, lighting
- Controllability of systems, thermal comfort
- Thermal comfort, design

- Daylight & views, daylight 75% of spaces
- Daylight & views, views for 90% of space

Sustainable Sites

A maximum of 14 points are devoted to this criteria. The perquisite for credit is that construction activity has prevented pollution. The project has been developed on a site that is considered to be sustainable. Existing buildings and/or sites are being reused. Natural and agricultural areas are being protected. The site is accessed by public transportation, reducing the need for automobile use. Natural sites within the project site or adjacent have been protected and/or restored. One point is assigned to each of the following checklist items:

- Site selection
- Development Density and Community Connectivity
- Brownfield Development
- Alternative Transportation -Public
- Alternative Transportation - Bicycle Storage
- Alternative Transportation – Low Emitting and Fuel Efficient

Vehicles

- Alternative Transportation – Parking Capacity
- Site Development – Protect or Restore Habitat
- Site Development – Maximize Open Space
- Storm Water Design – Quantity Control
- Storm Water Design – Quality Control
- Heat Island Effect – Non Roof
- Heat Island Effect – Roof
- Light Pollution Reduction

Water Efficiency

A maximum of 5 points are devoted to this criteria. The quantity of water required for the building has been reduced. The burden that the building imposes on municipal water supply and treatment has been reduced. One point is assigned to each of the following checklist items:

- Water Efficient Landscaping, Reduce by 50%

- Water Efficient Landscaping, No Potable Use or No Irrigation
- Innovative Wastewater Technologies
- Water Use Reduction, 20% Reduction
- Water Use Reduction, 30% Reduction

Energy and Atmosphere
A maximum of 17 points are devoted to this criteria. The building systems provide for energy efficiency, at optimum levels. The use of renewable and alternative energy sources has been encouraged. Ozone protection protocols have been supported. Points are awarded as follows:

- Optimize Energy Performance – Up to 10 points is provided depending on percentage of the new or rehabilitated building meets these criteria. The scale of percentages is provided in the GBCI checklist. For example, one credit is awarded for 14% in new buildings, and ten credits are awarded for 38.5% in new buildings.
- On-Site Renewable Energy – up to three credits are awarded based on percentages achieved. For example, at 2.5% renewable energy, one credit is awarded, but at 12.5 % renewable energy, the full three credits are awarded.
- Enhanced Commissioning – one point.
- Enhanced Refrigerant Management – one point
- Measurement & Verification – one point.

Materials and Resources
Up to 13 points are awarded for this category. Materials and resources are used that have less of an environmental impact. Waste is reduced and managed. The amount of materials used is reduced. One point is assigned to each of the following checklist items:

- Storage & Collection of Recyclables
- Building Reuse, Maintain 75% of Existing Walls, Floors & Roof
- Building Reuse, Maintain 95% of Existing Walls, Floors & Roof
- Building Reuse, Maintain 50% of Interior Non-Structural Elements

- Construction Waste Management, Divert 50% from Disposal
- Construction Waste Management, Divert 75% from Disposal
- Materials Reuse, 10%
- Recycled Content, 10% (post-consumer + 1/2 pre-consumer)
- Recycled Content, 20% (post-consumer + 1/2 pre-consumer)
- Regional Materials, 10% Extracted, Processed & Manufactured
- Regional Materials, 20% Extracted, Processed & Manufactured
- Rapidly Renewable Materials
- Certified Wood

The LEED 2009 Green Building Rating System awarded points toward certification as follows:

- ☐ Certified 40–49 points
- ☐ Silver 50–59 points
- ☐ Gold 60–79 points
- ☐ Platinum 80 points and above

GBCI will recognize buildings that achieve one of these rating levels with a formal letter of certification. In the evaluation to determine if a building will be LEED certified, a points system is utilized. In 2010, LEED consisted of a suite of nine rating systems for the design, construction and operation of buildings, homes and neighborhoods. Five overarching categories correspond to the specialties available under the LEED Accredited Professional program. That suite currently consists of:

Green Building Design & Construction
- LEED for New Construction and Major Renovations
- LEED for Core & Shell Development
- LEED for Schools
- LEED for Retail New Construction (planned 2010)

Green Interior Design & Construction
- LEED for Commercial Interiors
- LEED for Retail Interiors (planned 2010)

Green Building Operations & Maintenance
- LEED for Existing Buildings: Operations & Maintenance

Green Neighborhood Development
- LEED for Neighborhood Development

Green Home Design and Construction
- LEED for Homes

Given budget constraints for capital projects, there is some resistance to pursuing LEED certification by some agencies and Owners. When LEED certification is pursued, the cost of construction and initial design is higher than it would be without building for LEED certification. Sometimes in government, capital costs are not always looked at in tandem with future operating costs. There are, after all, distinct capital budgets and facility operating budgets.

Some designers may not have a high level of experience designing for LEED or to simply provide a LEED standard, even with more experience, a higher level of service by design professionals is required.

There can also be scarcity in the market for building components that meet LEED standards, and therefore they are more expensive than alternatives that might be used for a non LEED certified facility. There are also the added costs associated with the certification process itself, and the hiring of a commissioning authority required for completing the process.

Of course, the cost savings that will accrue even with these higher initial costs have proven that those costs are mitigated over time, when operational costs are lowered. There are other forms of payback, not easily measured, such as increased employee productivity working in a healthier building.

Examples of LEED Certified Public Projects

Let's look at a project that demonstrates how its Owner, the City of New York, was able to achieve LEED Silver Certification:

The Bronx Library Center
Bronx, New York.

This new construction project received LEED Silver Certification in 2006. This was achieved through the award of 34 points, out of a possible 69 points:

- Sustainable Sites 7/14
- Water Efficiency 3/5
- Energy & Atmosphere 3/17
- Materials & Resources 7/13
- Indoor Environmental Quality 9/15
- Innovation & Design 5/5

This project was the first New York City municipal building to achieve LEED certification. It was built at a cost of $53 million, at five stories and 178,000 square feet. The building it replaced was about one third of its size. Some of the features that led to LEED Silver certification included the following:

- A glass curtainwall that allows daylight into much of the library made from high performance glass and insulated frames. Translucent shades and other features supported the building's successful use of natural light.
- Photosenors and occupancy sensors conserve energy by turning off lights in rooms that are not occupied, or where there is sufficient daylight.
- The roofing system reflects solar heat, thus limiting the project's contribution to urban heat island effect, and reducing internal cooling loads.
- Outside air is used for cooling. The energy efficient strategies incorporated into the sign anticipated a reduction in energy costs by 20%.
- Materials were selected by the design team based on their environmental characteristics. This included recycled materials for the foundation, structural steel, carpeting, terrazzo and linoleum flooring. 80% of the wood used in the library, based on cost, was certified to Forest Stewardship Council Standards.

- The paints, adhesives and sealants produce low chemical emissions, and composite wood products have no added urea-formaldehyde.
- More than half of the building materials were manufactured within 500 miles of the site, and a recycling plan diverted 90% of all construction and demolition waste from the landfill.

Joe Serna Jr. California EPA Headquarters Building Sacramento, California

This state project, a rehabilitation of an existing facility, received a LEED Platinum 60 rating. Upon completion, the building became 34% more energy efficient, and has diverted more than 200 tons of waste from landfills each year. This was achieved in 2003 through the award of 60 points out of a possible 75 points:

- Sustainable Sites 13/16
- Water Efficiency 3/5
- Energy & Atmosphere 20/22
- Materials & Resources 10/10
- Indoor Environmental
- Quality 12/18
- Innovation & Design 2/5

This rehabilitation was a relatively small project. The building's Owner invested $500,000 in efficiency upgrades to equipment, operations and employee practices. These improvements generated $610,000 in annual savings, paying for themselves in less than one year. Using an 8% capitalization rate, the annual cost savings have increased the asset value of the building by nearly $12 million. LEED Platinum was achieved by:

- Increasing water and energy efficiency and reducing waste disposal costs
- Utilizing native, drought resistant grasses, plants and trees to minimize storm water runoff and reduce heat building
- Installation of low-flow toilets, water free urinals, and water efficient fixtures, decreasing exterior water use by 50% and interior water use by 220%

- Installation of a highly efficient HVAC and lighting system, photovoltaic rooftop panels and a plate and frame heat exchanger that reduces on/off cycling of the chiller equipment
- Elimination of garbage can liners and using reusable cloth bags in centrally located recycling bins
- Allowing for more than 80% of the office space to be filled with natural light

As caretakers of the public trust, agency managers and administrators have the opportunity to continue to substantially contribute to sustainable development by seeking training as LEED certified professionals, and seeking green design initiatives of the Architect / Engineer in order to create construction documents that promote green building. Targeting projects for LEED certification incentifies the project team to make extraordinary efforts to achieve sustainable development goals.

Sustainable development has come to the fore in response to traditional ways of construction and development, which practiced unsustainable development in the consumption of the earth's natural resources, land use, and resultant waste and pollution. As a result of legislation and education, sustainable development has been embraced by agencies that manage public works, as well as other Owners who development the land. Federal, state and local laws and regulations, as well as zoning regulations have addressed land use, construction means and methods in order to promote sustainability and to control density across the land. Best Management Practices have created the structures and systems to control pollution, such as sedimentation in storm water runoff during construction operations.

The public sector has begun to embrace sustainability, and many current design and construction management solicitations now address goals for **Leadership in Energy and Environmental Design (LEED).**

Chapter 11 References

The following sources were utilized in writing this chapter

Kiebert, C. Editor, Reshaping the Built Environment. 1999. Island Press. Washington, DC.

Kibert, C.J. & Sendzimir, J & Guy, B (2002) *Construction Ecology: Nature as a basis for green buildings*. London and New York: Spon Press

National Environmental Policy Act.
http://www.epa.gov/compliance/nepa/

Sustainable City Government Partnership. Portland Oregon DOT.
http://www.portlandonline.com/transportation/index.cfm?print=1&a=301433&c=34753

Sustainability Guidelines. Construction Management Association of America. 2010
United Nations Conference on Sustainable Development.
http://www.un.org/esa/sustdev/documents/agenda21/english/Agenda21.pdf

United States Green Building Council. Retrieved from:
http://www.usgbc.org/

Al Palumbo

Chapter 12
Leadership

Leadership is the ability to understand people and empowering them to help you do a job. That takes all of the good characteristics, like integrity, dedication of purpose, selflessness, knowledge, skill, implacability, as well as determination not to accept failure.

~Admiral Arleigh A. Burke

Leadership

In writing this textbook, a common thread that I tried to weave into most of the book is "leadership". In construction, as in any endeavor, leadership motivates individuals to come together, work as a team, and accomplish a goal or objective.

Who is a Leader?

Leaders have a vision. They see a problem within the organization that has not been attended to, and needs fixing; or they set a goal that needs to be achieved to make the organization better. Once they arrive at this awareness, they become determined to go after the objective.

In the private sector, my objective was to triple and quadruple my company's annual revenue, even in a recession and downtown in the local construction market. The only way for me to achieve that goal was to elevate the level of service my firm provided by recruiting and hiring motivated, skilled and experienced construction professionals.

Good work gets more work, and this is the golden rule of developing and building a construction consulting business. The leader always has a target right in front that looms large.

The "vision thing", a phrase borrowed from president George H.W. Bush, is not enough. Many people become aware that things need to be fixed, and that goals need to be achieved, but only leaders step forward, because they are different. They act and react, to get where the organization needs to go. When leaders motivate subordinates, and their subordinates in turn motivate their departments, divisions and staff units to respond, leadership transfers to them because they share the goal, set new goals, and do their part to meet the organization's objectives.

All leaders have similar traits and characteristics that make them leaders. The first is integrity. Those that are led believe that the leader is not ego driven, but trying to do what is right. The leader also accepts the people that are being led for who they are. Everyone is different, and everyone can contribute in a unique way. The leader wants subordinates to contribute, and for them to have a sense of self worth. Employees have a sense of purpose and want to come to work every day and contribute. Leaders understand that people in the organization need to be encouraged and rewarded for their contributions and accomplishments. The leader does not dwell on the negative, but accentuates the positive. He or she doesn't waste time telling you want you are doing wrong, but works with you to get it right.

Finally, the leader knows how to communicate in order to motivate people to achieve the goal. Everyone has a trigger that when pulled motivates them to achieve. A leader knows when to pull the trigger, without getting lost in the details, focusing on the higher objective. The leader knows how to "keep it moving".

Leadership in the Public Agency

I have worked for more than 35 years in public agencies and for private for profit engineering and construction firms, and during my tenure I have witnessed leadership styles ranging from strong leadership, poor leadership and no leadership on construction projects. I have seen public agency managers allow their projects to stall, fall behind schedule, allow quality to slip, allow rancor and negativity on the project site. I have also witnessed strong leadership, with a motivated workforce, cooperation with contractors, partnerships between the Agency and the Construction

Manager and design team. In projects of this type, the Construction Manager was fair but firm with the contractors, and was respected for that reason. The Construction Manager was able to lead because the Agency allowed it and demanded it.

Everything that I said here about leadership is multi-dimensional. It is at the Agency level, it is at the stakeholder level, and it is the Agency's team of professional engineers, architects, and construction management partners.

Without naming any names, I can tell you that you can hire a construction management firm that has a standing within the Engineering News Record's top 10 in the United States, but the size and reputation of that firm doesn't matter if they don't give you the "A Team". Experienced and inexperienced Project Managers, whether at the Agency or consultant level, can exhibit poor leadership. They can harass, berate, blame, cajole, or hide in their office. Fortunately for me, I have come across some great leaders in this industry, which exude integrity and confidence, and get the Agency's business done.

As I stated at the outset, leadership is first and foremost exercised at the Agency level. Following suit, the Construction Manager must also have the leadership qualities to focus the workforce on the project, the schedule, the budget, and quality. These are the goals and objectives that the project leader must seek to meet.

At the highest level, the leader of a construction agency should want the Agency to be an example of excellence, in all aspects of the mission. At all supervisory levels, management should be infused with a leadership style that sets goals for every component of the Agency's delivery system.

Public agencies either self perform or direct consultants to perform design and construction management services. Whether the Project Manager is employed directly by Agency or is hired by the Construction Manager, the leader's mission is to have subordinates buy into the vision and goals of the project. The primary mission is a project delivered safely, on time, and within the budget. I am a strong advocate of a strong leadership style at the Agency and field level. As one of my former bosses used to say, "Nothing happens by magic!" Planning, strategy, a positive environment, a motivated workforce, and the drive to get the job done is the magic that is created by a leader that drives the project and makes everyone associated with it proud of what they are accomplishing.

Exercising Leadership

If you are in a position to shape the direction of the Agency's projects, then provide the public service of exercising leadership. Do this by ensuring that your subordinates understand the processes in place to do the job. Process is one of the most important aspects of public administration. It establishes the norms, protocols and the rules. Make sure that your staff has full knowledge of the project plans and specifications, and the technical processes involved in the construction of your project.

Maintain the integrity of the process in procurement, bid and award of contracts. Select the best and most qualified firms to complete the project on time, within budget, safety and with quality.

Ensure that management systems are in place to monitor time and budget, and that there is a mechanism to react to the red flags proactively to bring the project in on time and within budget.

Implement quality control and quality assurance through a rigorous program of on site daily inspection of the work, testing, strict control of submittals and quick responses by the Architect/Engineer in the review of submittals, issuances of clarifications, and interpretation of the construction documents.

Get what you pay for from the Construction Manager. Demand leadership, management and control of the project site, a safe project, and a positive project environment for the completion of the project.

Use your project as a vehicle to promote the growth of small businesses, especially within the community. Carve out opportunities for small businesses, including WBEs, DBEs, and MBEs, to perform and grow from the experience. Don't just set goals, but go the extra mile and advocate for these firms by creating networking and procurement opportunities, providing business assistance and mentoring.

Promote sustainability and green building design. Seek LEED certification for your project. Invest in projects that will have a payback to the public in operations and maintenance and saving natural resources. Don't just look at the cost of construction. Think about the cost of operation for years to come, and how smart decisions will provide an incredible payback over time.

Demand a safe project. Make sure that safety trumps everything. Encourage your design team to think outside the box when it comes to safety by practicing safety by design. Safety shouldn't just be reactive and it shouldn't just be the responsibility of the contractor. There are pro-active measures at small cost that can save millions, as well as grief and heartache.

Let your team do their jobs. Don't micro-manage them. Provide the vision and leadership to guide them, and let them go to work to accomplish the project.

Always get what you pay for. The Agency is entitled to the design that you approved long before the start of construction. Be firm in expecting what is required, and exercise your rights as well as your responsibilities.

"Public service is the noblest of professions if it's done honorably, if it's done right...It's an aphrodisiac, in a way. Once you've done it, there's nothing comparable."

Edward I. Koch – Former Mayor
City of New York

Al Palumbo

ABOUT THE AUTHOR

I began my career as an employment and training specialist for a federal jobs program. With a degree in American history and secondary education, I never expected that I would spend 30 years in the construction industry. My introduction to construction was in the office of New York City Mayor Ed Koch. There, I was in charge of investigating and auditing labor law and training requirements tied to contracts between the city agencies and construction contractors. Knowing next to nothing about construction, this is when I first realized that I could use a book like this one. After that, I went to work for a public benefit corporation, holding the positions of principal construction contract administrator and Owner's representative for the reconstruction of state funded middle income housing, where I assisted in managing a $500 million construction defect repair program.

In the private sector, I worked as a vice president for several engineering and construction management consulting firms, and I also formed a company to co-develop an affordable housing project with state and municipal funding in East Harlem, NY. I earned an MBA in construction management, became a certified construction manager through the Construction Management Institute of the CMAA, and an authorized OSHA trainer. My last public agency job was as director of operations and capital programs for a large municipal agency in New York City. I am presently employed as a career counselor and trainer for City University of New York Research Foundation, and stay involved in construction as a consultant with a design and build general contractor, assisting them in growing and managing their business.

I live in Brooklyn, NY with my wife Anna, and listen to my daughter, Cristina, on Sirius XM radio, where she works as an on-air personality and associate producer.

www.ingramcontent.com/pod-product-compliance
Lightning Source LLC
Chambersburg PA
CBHW061505180526
45171CB00001B/37